ENEMIES AND OBSESSIONS

ENEMIES AND OBSESSIONS

MORE MEMORIES AND MUSINGS

Raymond Apple

emeritus rabbi of the Great Synagogue, Sydney

authorHOUSE®

AuthorHouse™ UK Ltd.
1663 Liberty Drive
Bloomington, IN 47403 USA
www.authorhouse.co.uk
Phone: 0800.197.4150

Published by AuthorHouse   10/03/2014

ISBN: 978-1-4969-9223-9 (sc)
ISBN: 978-1-4969-9225-3 (e)

CONTENTS

FOREWORD

In my book of memoirs I tell the story of how long and hard I looked for a title until my friend Rabbi Yitzhack Rubin suggested "To Be Continued". I guess that when I adopted Yitz's suggestion I must have had a vague inkling that one day I would write another instalment.

The pattern of "To Be Continued" was thematic: about a hundred short chapters, in alphabetical order, on themes that had characterised my life and career. I am not certain how many copies of the initial print run were sold, though the reception accorded to the book was quite warm and favourable. I had no expectation of any royalties and the book made me no money. Actually hardly any of my books brought me any income, but that was never my purpose in writing.

Now that I have penned a rather brief sequel to "To Be Continued" I have to be honest and say that the pleasure I derived from thinking back, chuckling at the memory and feeding a new series of thoughts into the computer is my best reward. Nonetheless I hope that those who read the book will enjoy it, and that too will be a reward.

This time there is no logical sequence in the material. It is not classified alphabetically or by any other criterion. Though it reflects events in my life, it records thoughts and themes in the order in which they entered my mind. I make no attempt at drawing out of them or any other pieces of evidence of my activities or attitudes a consistent philosophy of life. I may even have contradicted myself here and there. I hope I may paraphrase a far greater writer who said, "Do I contradict myself? Well then, I contradict myself".

By the time this short book appears I will, please God, be on the way to my eightieth year. I am conscious that the Pir'kei Avot say at the end of Chapter 5, *Ben shemonim lig'vurah* – "At eighty for special strength". According to one school of thought, that dictum is to be taken as a euphemism, and what the author really meant to say, but may have been too polite to voice it so explicitly, was "At eighty you are decrepit and diminishing". Fortunately, another view says, "If you are eighty, God has given you a gift of life and health, and you have to use it with energy and gratitude". I'm not certain which interpretation applies in my case, but I pray to God that it may be the second. In which case I once again echo Yitz Rubin and say, "To Be Continued".

- RAYMOND APPLE

This book was sponsored by Ros and Alex Fischl and Sue and Jake Selinger

1

JOBS I COULD HAVE HAD

I was fortunate in my congregations. I hope they felt fortunate in me. Yet at moments of frustration I thought of moving into another area, possibly the law. By the next day, however, I usually felt better and decided to stay in the rabbinate. But there were occasions when I was approached in relation to rabbinic or communal vacancies, and this is the story of some of them.

Before leaving Australia, a top post in the Zionist movement was offered to me. I was tempted, but I had my passage booked for overseas, hoping to come back as director of the United Jewish Education Board in Melbourne. In England I was offered the job of head of Hebrew studies at a Jewish school, but I decided to stay in the ministry. I once applied for the post of principal of a south coast school but did not rate an interview. Dr. Epstein asked if I would take extra degrees in order to become head of the Jews' College teachers' faculty but I declined. In later years I was acting director of the NSW Board of Jewish Education and taught at the Guild Teachers' College, but the pulpit remained my main career.

Work with students was always high on my agenda. I considered becoming director of the Hillel Foundation in Britain whilst retaining the Hampstead pulpit, but the double pressures would have been too much. I had already been sounded out about being Hillel Director in Sydney, with training in the USA, but again I decided to remain in the ministry.

Ministerial positions were offered in a number of countries. To get me to the USA I was told, "With your British accent you could earn $18,000 a year". It was a large sum in those days, and my accent was rather British, but I was worried about the lack of security in the American rabbinate. I was asked about a job in South Africa but then I asked, "Can my wife go for a walk in the street at night?" Other offers ranged from New Zealand to Finland, Ireland and many parts of England. When Chief Rabbi Jakobovits told me about a difficult community in the Provinces I said, "Thankyou, but I prefer to stay in Hampstead – I have no aggravation here!" The Chief retorted, "That's why I want you to go – aggravation would do you good!"

I didn't do what he wanted, but I did go to Sydney and had times of aggravation, not so much in the Synagogue but in the rabbinate generally. At one stage my name was placed without my knowledge on a list of possible candidates for Chief Rabbi of Britain but I had a lucky escape.

I was offered a full-time university post; again I opted for the pulpit, and I had to wait until I retired in order to devote myself to scholarship, though I did have many happy years as a part-time university lecturer.

2

THEATRICS

When women began to seek public expressions of spirituality, Rav Moshe Feinstein was not totally opposed like some lesser authorities. He said it all depended on the women's motivation. If true love of God moved them there could be areas of approval, but not if their purpose was to make a statement.

I apply the distinction to men as well. Those who constantly seek new *ḥumrot* (stringencies) need to be asked, are you motivated by love of God and the yearning to intensify your religious experience? Or are you making a statement? What moves you – piety or theatrics?

A case in point – "*tzitzis arois*" or "*oisgehangene tzitzis*". *Frum* men of an earlier generation all wore *tzitzit*. Not hanging outside their clothes. The *tzitzit* law in the *Sh'ma* says *ur'item oto*, "You shall look at it". "Looking" implies visibility. In the past, looking at the *tzitzit* happened privately when getting dressed. Things have now changed. Some non-Jews know these are "Jewish holy strings". The unpleasant comments come from fellow Jews.

What is the "*tzitzis arois*" motivation - genuine piety or mere theatrics: "Look at me, everybody – see how *frum* I am!" Is this an implied intolerance of others who don't share your opinion? Maybe the message is "See how un-*frum you* are!" The test of whether it is theatrics is provided by the *tzitzit*-text itself: "You shall look at it and remember all the commandments of the Lord and do them"... i.e., when you look at your *tzitzit* do you ask yourself, "How do I rate with the other commandments?"

There are three verbs here – *look, remember, do.* A sequence – *see, think, act.* You don't just see for seeing's sake. You see, so that your mind will be stimulated and your whole being will commit itself to right action. How do we define right action? The verse says, "Do not follow the desires of your heart and eyes which lead you astray". There are three types of desire – for food, money and sex. Heart and eyes tempt you in all three directions. Neither food, money or sex is bad in itself. Each has to be directed: neither denied nor deified but directed. Theatrics thinks of *tzitzit* as showing off. Genuine piety sees them as reminding us to direct and discipline our desires.

Early in my career I was hesitant about accepting an invitation to a Barmitzvah lunch on Shabbat in a congregant's home. The *ba'al simḥah* assured us, "We're *very* orthodox!" We didn't know how to respond. In the end we did attend, but for more objective reasons. The episode taught me a lesson, not to value too highly anyone's assertion, "Look how religious I am!" I'd rather that things spoke for themselves and that people could humbly say to God, "Look, *Avinu Shebashamayim*, we're really and truly trying to live by Your Word!"

3

A SEASON TICKET
FOR THE TORAH

The sages had an order of priorities for call-ups to the Torah: first the *kohen*, then the *levi*, then the rest of us. The system more or less worked, but what if there were too many *kohanim*, or too few – and the same with the *levi'im*? The surname Cohen doesn't always denote priestly background, nor do "Levi" or "Levy" guarantee levitical status. I knew a Mr. Cohen who was a *levi* and a Mr. Levy who was a *kohen*.

At the Great Synagogue in my time the main problem was what to do if there was only one *kohen* or one *levi*. Should the same people be called up every week? In time everyone knew that Jack Freedman would be called up first and Eric Levy second. The word was that they had season tickets.

Managing the *aliyot* requires great skill. Even with call-up lists drafted in advance, a resourceful *shammash* is vital. After our *shammas*, Bernat Kahan, retired, the Secretary, Norman Goodman, took over the role, tall and dignified in a top hat. The old-time *shammashim* in London Shules wore robes as well, and in one historic synagogue the *shammash* wore livery. For a while, teenage boys in academic gowns performed the role at the Great, and then a congregant, Steven Jurke, became "the singing *shammash*" and does a *haftarah* at the drop of a hat (though he has no topper). Latecomers, disgruntled congregants, visitors – all are woven into his spell.

Not that he – or any other *shammash* - can predict every eventuality. Such as a veteran member who starts his *b'rakhah* correctly but ends "*al achilat maror*" (the blessing for bitter herbs on Pesa<u>h</u>), and the *ba'al k'ri'ah* (me!) doesn't bat an eyelid, says, "Amen" and continues with the reading – even though he wants to collapse with laughter.

There are people who insist on "proper" call-ups. I hope they don't think some are improper. They have no idea that *hagbahah* and *gelilah* are the really superior *mitzvot* because they involve actually handling the scroll. The complainers claim that a "real" call-up entails saying a *b'rakhah*, though they can't always handle the Hebrew words. They'd be lost without the English transliteration, and some can't even read that. How often did I have to prompt the words? I could have said anything, even the blessing on leaving the toilet, and they wouldn't have known the difference.

There are those who have no Hebrew name or can't remember it. You need immense resourcefulness in such cases… How do you handle a congregant like one I had in London, who insisted that his Hebrew name was "William ben George"? If he were a member of the Royal Family it might work (though the latest royal baby is, theoretically, George ben William).

4

LAMED-VAV TZADDIKIM

It's a privilege to stand in the pulpit on Rosh HaShanah and Yom Kippur and marvel at the crowd. After some years a rabbi knows more or less everyone, and is aware of their often hidden qualities of heart, mind and soul, as well as the capacity so many have for love and courage.

This links up with the fascinating notion of the thirty-six hidden saints in each generation, the *Lamed-Vav Tzaddikim*. The idea has four tenets:

The world rests on righteousness, especially on righteous individuals; the righteous are often not aware of their own greatness: Moses "knew not that his face shone" (Ex. 34:35); if their greatness were known, the spell could be broken; each generation has 36 *tzaddikim*.

Andre Schwarz-Bart used the *Lamed-Vav* theme in his novel, *The Last of the Just* (1959). It depicts generations of virtue starting in the Middle Ages and ending with the Holocaust. The story is questionable. There is no proof that being a *Lamed-Vavnik* is an inherited trait which might terminate.

Prov. 10:25 calls the *tzaddik* the foundation of the world. The Talmud says every generation has *tzaddikim* who are as great as the patriarchs. How many are there in each age? The sages of Eretz Yisrael (Hullin 92a) say 30, the Babylonians (Sanh. 97b) say 36.

Why these multiples of six? Do they connect with the idea of *tzaddikim* being concealed? Perhaps the significance of 6 is that it is not 7. 7 is completeness, while 6 symbolises imperfection, like a week without Shabbat: in a sense the *tzaddik* is the Shabbat of the world. 36 is 6 sixes.

In Alexandrian Jewish philosophy, imperfection is 6 squared; astrology has 36 decans, each governing 10 degrees of the 360 degree zodiac. Medieval manuscripts give each one the name of a Biblical character.

The idea that the power of the righteous depends on their concealment is recent, though there were many modest *tzaddikim*. Gershom Scholem thinks the concept re-entered Judaism from Islam in the distinction between the "concealed" and "revealed" *tzaddik* and the Hassidic doctrine that anyone can have latent messianic potential. Hence one of the 36 *tzaddikim* of each age is the Mashiach, who will be revealed only if the generation is worthy.

A quiet unassuming person may be a *lamed-vavnik*: so may you or I. No-one is a nobody. Addressing a conference of doctors, Abraham Joshua Heschel said, "I feel humble in your presence. The least of you has to his credit the merit of soothing pain, of preventing grief and tears" (*The Insecurity of Freedom*, 1966). When I looked at my Holyday congregation, I felt humble in their presence. The least of them had deep religiosity of heart, mind and spirit.

5

THE PERSON OR THE NOISE

A school inspector told my class that "history" was really "his story".
I forgive his sexism but not his etymology. The word is actually from the
Greek "*historein*", to see, enquire, account or narrate ("*histor*" = a judge).
But in one sense he did have a point, in that much of history is what people
were and did. As a child I read *Van Loon's Lives*, which records history that
is not primarily economic, political, cultural, ideological and geographical,
but also biographical. So, back to Greek origins. "*Bios*" means life (hence
words such as biology, biochemistry, etc.), and "*graphein*" is to write.

Biography is hard to write. Its focus is on a life or lives. It was said of
Hitler: "That man does not exist. He is only the noise he makes". So I ask
every biographer, "What are you writing about – the person or the noise?"

My own experience as a biographer is mostly of rabbis and intellectuals,
British, German and Australian. I have even written a personal memoir (*To
Be Continued*, published 2010), not out of vanity but to ponder my areas
of activity. Its sequel is *Enemies and Obsessions*, the present book. I have
learned a few things *en route*. I call them "Warnings to the Biographer":

- You may not always like the person you are writing about, but let
  the sources speak for themselves - and place the person in their
  context.
- There are extremes to avoid – the one is *tokhehah*: revenge or
  punishment; the other is *hesped*: fulsome flattery or whitewashing.

Alexander Marx says in his *Essays in Jewish Biography* (1947): "I have striven, as far as it is humanly possible, to present an objective picture... not permitting my personal feelings of admiration or intimate friendship to blind my judgment". Good advice. The question is, "Did the person I wrote about really exist, or was it all just noise?" Does one see what Israel Zangwill called "pages filled with coloured pictures?" Depicting people's lives is easier in relation to an earlier age because so much of the material is extant. These days people don't write letters any more (because of computers, a lack of manners or time, or both?) But can one write biography without files of letters and bundles of papers? We have diminishing source material – and emails help little, since most get trashed when an inbox begins to burst.

In Jewish biography, how do we measure the way a person flitted in and out of their Jewish identity? Or the impact of their environment? Some Jewish biographers want to preach a sermon on pride in one's heritage. As a preacher I am tempted to follow that view: as a historian I have a different role. I have to paint what my eyes see, and not let my dreams brush it up. It's not easy.

6

GO TO THE DEVIL

I was never very good at blowing the *shofar*, though when I was leaving the Bayswater Synagogue I trained the Shule Secretary to take over as *ba'al teki'ah*. Some of the congregation decided that when I struggled with the notes, Satan was in the way. A case of "the devil's in the detail"? Actually, Jews don't believe in the devil, named Satan or anything else. I know that missionaries warn that if we reject Christianity we will go to the devil, but the threat holds no fears for us. The devils we know are generally humans.

In Tanakh, Satan as a noun is an adversary (of any kind); as a verb, it denotes to oppose or be hostile. Sometimes Scripture uses it in a human sense. In Psalm 109:6, Zechariah 3 and Job, it is the counsel for the prosecution - but the name is symbolic and does not denote a real being or God's enemy. At worst Satan is a devil's advocate who draws God's attention to human failings. Kaufmann Kohler calls Satan an allegorical figure "representing the evil of the world, both physical and moral".

Post-Biblical references to Satan are hyperbole without theological status, e.g. "Don't go on a journey with a wicked man, because Satan accompanies him", or simply, "Do not give Satan an opening". The Midrash blames Satan for the golden calf and for David's sin with Bathsheba. *Satan Mekatreg*, "Satan the Accuser", alleging that Abraham, Job and other pious people are not quite what they seem, is a colourful metaphor, not an actual being. Ideas that he is a former angel who has turned against God are not to be taken literally. That's why, when the *ba'al teki'ah* can't get a note out of the *shofar*, some say that *Satan Mekatreg* is in the instrument. The

11

prayerbook asks God to "remove the adversary from before us and behind us",and for protection from "the destroying adversary". Folklore urged people to avoid evil spirits in wasteland or cemeteries.

Christian folk thinking, on the other hand, took seriously the idea of a demon entering a human being and needing to be exorcised. In sectarian writings and ideologies such as Zoroastrianism, the devil or demons are enemies of God. The Christian notion of a being who is opposed to God and to Jesus appealed to the poet John Milton. In the early books of his *Paradise Lost* he makes Satan a presiding demon who is almost an epic hero. Later Milton reduced Satan's stature and expected him to be overcome, hence the theme of *Paradise Regained*. Rebellious angels are found in late Kabbalah, but not as normative doctrine. Nonetheless Satan as a symbol is present throughout history. What havoc is wrought when satanic forces get hold of supposedly civilised people and make them threaten the survival of humanity and demonise those with whom they disagree!

7

A BIRTHDAY IS NO HOLIDAY

I don't make a fuss about birthdays though I know how important they were in my childhood. Though I don't have the old energy and resilience, I hope I have grown in wisdom. It is highly flattering to hear that someone said of me recently, "Rabbi Apple is the wisest man I have met".

Back to birthdays. Mendele Mocher Sefarim said, "For Jews a birthday is no holiday: but the anniversary of a death, that a Jew remembers". This possibly reflects the view of Kohelet (7:1), "The day of death is better than the day of birth". According to the Midrash, birth and death are like two ships in the harbour. Why rejoice over the ship that is setting out on a voyage? No-one knows what storms lie ahead. Everyone should however rejoice to see a ship returning to port. In my opinion even the first ship should be greeted. A ship that sets out may register new finds and new types of paradise. Everyone should wish it well. Even if all it does is to navigate the waters calmly and travel smoothly, that is already an achievement.

The birth of a baby is an occasion for hope, since every child brings a new blessing with it. Regardless of Mendele, birthdays should be a *yomtov*.

Why is there only one birthday in the Torah –Pharaoh's? It can't be that villains like Pharaoh really deserve congratulations. Why does the Mishnah Avodah Zarah note the birthdays of the Roman and other gentile kings, harsh rulers with very little feeling for their people? The explanation is probably prosaic. Kings' birthdays were matters of record, whilst for ordinary people there was no registration system. Parents knew what time of year their child was born, but the exact date was hard to remember.

There are people who arbitrarily fix on a date for their birthday and some who consciously distort the truth. The novelist Benjamin Leopold Farjeon, according to Harry Kellerman, changed his birthday from December to May "because May falls at a better time of the year".

Certain anniversaries had religious consequences, such as religious majority, 13 for a boy, 12 for a girl, and becoming 60, when the Biblical punishment of *karet* ("excision") no longer applied, because one view said it symbolised dying young. Some people echoed Jer. 20:14, "Cursed be the day I was born" – but it was not so much a (possibly superstitious) prejudice against a particular date as a pessimistic comment on life in general.

Later rabbis like the Ben Ish Hai had a positive attitude to birthdays. The Hafetz Hayyim saw each year as a reward for guarding one's tongue. The Tz'dakah LaHayyim recommended intensifying one's Torah study, prayer and charity on their birthday. On his birthday the K'tav Sofer had a *siyyum* (conclusion of a Talmudic tractate).

8

CHICKEN OR THE EGG

Our belief in Creation postulates a simple story: yesterday there was nothing, today there is a world, and since worlds do not come out of the blue, there must have been a Creator who was responsible for making everything exist. That's all very well when we consider the stones, rocks and other inanimate elements in Nature: first there was nothing, then there were stones and rocks. What about things that have the capacity to change, grow, develop and generate other things?

Did God create readymade chickens with the capacity to produce eggs, or eggs with the capacity to become chickens and then produce more eggs? In other words, which came first, the chicken or the egg? Did God create Adam and Eve as fully-fledged reproductive beings, or was it foetuses or babies He created, with the inherent capacity to grow and become reproductive adults?

Maybe the 20th century figure of Superman is an endeavour to tackle the issue, in that Superman began as Superboy and then grew up – but Superboy did have parents in the planet from which he came. However, if Adam also had parents, then Adam was not Adam, but his father was!

There is a rabbinic passage in Pir'kei Avot chapter 5 (with other versions in Talmud Pesahim 54a and elsewhere), which speaks of ten miraculous things created at twilight on the first Sabbath eve. To the list is appended the statement, "Some say, also the tongs made with tongs". Is this saying meant to tease us, or does it have a serious import? The truth goes with the second option. As Israel Abrahams said, the ancient rabbis were not fantastic fools but serious philosophers. They asked homely questions, but their minds were sharp and searching. The reference to the tongs implies the question of which came first – the tongs (symbolic of instruments and tools)… or the tongs that made the tongs?

The general rabbinic answer is that there had to be a first step, an original set of tongs, and these were the work of the Creator. This in itself does not tell us whether Adam began as an adult or a baby, but he could not have been a mere foetus since then he would have been reliant on his mother, nor could he have been a baby, since babies do not bring themselves up.

The sages have a theory that Adam was created as a mature reproductive being, 20 years of age (Gen. R. 14:7), and the other creations also came into being fully developed: "All the works of creation were brought into being in a completed state" (R.H. 11a, Hullin 60a, Num. R. 12:8). There is a similar view in Greek and Roman literature.

9

MEZUZAH ON THE DOORPOST

The verse, "Write them (the words of the *Sh'ma*) on the doorposts of your house and on your gates" (Deut. 6:9), is the basis of the law of *mezuzah*.

I was once asked whether a long-term Jewish prisoner in gaol needed a *mezuzah* on his cell door and though I could find arguments in favour of affixing a *mezuzah* without a *b'rakhah*, the prison authorities would not allow it. They said that inmates can be moved from prison to prison and having to worry about a *mezuzah* would complicate the authorities' lives.

Rabbi Yona Metzger, when chief rabbi of Israel, ruled that a yacht in the Tel Aviv marina needed *mezuzot* if people were on board long enough for it to be their dwelling place; likewise with ocean-going liners and cruise ships. It is different if you are crossing a river in a canoe, or going across a harbour on a ferry, paddle steamer or something similar, because no "dwelling" is involved. *Rambam (Hil'khot Mezuzah 6:9)* applies this exemption to a *sukkah*, even though the Torah specifies, "*Basukkot tesh'vu shiv'at yamim* – you shall dwell in *sukkot* for seven days" (Lev. 23:42). An elevator does not need a *mezuzah* (though some rabbis take a different view) because it is constantly on the go and has no permanent lateral location. A yacht or cruise ship also moves, but people use its facilities like their home.

Why is a *mezuzah* important? It is a mark of Jewish identity; a way to express one's Jewishness, like the Hebrews in ancient Egypt who placed blood on their doorposts (Ex. 12:7): but it is far more than a mere token of identity. It symbolises a commitment. Like Jonah who said, "I am a Hebrew and I fear the Lord" (Jonah 1:9), the *mezuzah* says, "I am Jewish, and my home stands for Jewish belief, practice and principles".

Other outward signs of commitment are circumcision (on the body) and *tzitzit* (on the clothes). Taken together, they show dedication of one's world to the word of God. The *mezuzah* bears the Hebrew letters *shin-dalet-yod*, short for "*Shaddai* – The Almighty". This, according to the sages, indicates that God specially protects the people who keep His commandments.

Hopefully Rabbi Metzger's ruling will help to ensure Divine protection for people who sail the seas. It applies – quite literally - the command of the *Shema* to remember God's word wherever we go. The Biblical wording speaks of "when you walk by the way"; these days walking by the way must certainly include flying in the air and sailing the seas.

At the Great Synagogue we were constantly finding that vandals or thieves were removing the *mezuzah* from the street entrance of the education and administrative centre. We gouged out a piece of the stonework so that we could insert a new *mezuzah* that would be flush with the doorway.

10

I'M BECOMING A DINOSAUR

I am worried about myself. It's not that I am faced – God forbid – by some looming spectre. It's a question of what I represent in a changing world. I fear I am becoming a dinosaur, a survival from an age that no longer exists.

Morbid thoughts like these began 50 years ago in London. An official of the United Synagogue Burial Society liked the way I conducted funerals (what a way to judge a man's capacity!). At Willesden Cemetery one day he said to me, "You remind me of the great Anglo-Jewish ministers of the past". I must have been developing a *gravitas* that didn't fit into a new age. (Someone else said I had an austere fervour, not to be mistaken for a fever).

This wasn't the first time I had experienced this problem. When I was only 15 or so, I wrote a few articles for the youth pages of a Melbourne daily paper. They decided to run an interview with me. They told their readers – at that stage it was quite true – that I planned to enter the diplomatic corps. They also said I was "pleasantly grave". Were they to know that, years later, graves – in quite another sense – would play such a role in my career?

My life seems to have been constantly marked by gravity, *gravitas*, dignity. It's out of date these days. But it's even worse. I also have an outdated sense of trying to use the judicious word and not do harm with my tongue, plus a debater's feeling that there may be truth on both sides of an argument. And some manners: "Is it a convenient moment to talk?"… "I hope you don't mind"… "I just wanted to say thankyou"… "Do you think this would be a good idea?"… "I'm not sure this would be politic"…

I try never to tell people they are liars. I prefer a method I learned from a London congregant who was a company director (the name of the company does not matter and in any case that particular company has probably been taken over or disappeared or both). At a board meeting he was quite sure the chairman was taking liberties with the truth. He could have said, "Mr. Chairman, you are an outrageous liar!" What he said instead was, "Mr. Chairman, I tend to think you have permitted yourself to be misinformed"…

I don't worship the past, despite being a historian. I don't fear the future, even though some trends of today will cause harm in time to come. I worry about the present when we seem to be so short of high-minded leadership. I confess to being an idealist and to believing in the honest and decent way of doing things. If I am wrong I will apologise in the world to come.

Someone in Sydney told me, "Your problem is that you think the way to get anywhere is the straight line from A to B, and you're not interested in deviousness." Maybe he was right. The little geometry I remember gave me a love of straight lines. Is that's what's making me a dinosaur?

11

PLURALISM AND PLURALITY

"Two Jews – three opinions" is a fact of life that goes even further than Elijah's "How long will you hesitate between two opinions?" It resonated through the ages, with dissident sects, competing ideologies, bitter conflicts and reluctant compromises. There has always been diversity. Even the problem of orthodox v. non-orthodox is not a modern invention. It's not whether the question is new, but whether anyone knows how to solve it.

Rabbi Joseph B. Soloveitchik distinguished between *b'rit goral*, the covenant of fate binding all Jews regardless of their opinions, and *b'rit Sinai*, the covenant of faith uniting those who uphold the Revelation on Sinai. It is a useful distinction, but it creates its own problems.

The second arm of the thesis allows Orthodoxy to maintain Sinai-based *halakhic* Judaism as the authentic tradition which defines a Jew, but leaves undecided the status of Conservative Judaism, which also claims to be *halakhic*, and of Reform, which whilst not claiming to be a *halakhic* position often claims *halakhic* legitimacy on the basis of a statement that both Bet Hillel and Bet Shammai are "the words of the living God".

Secular Jews come within *b'rit goral* but not *b'rit Sinai*, and do not make any claims to "the words of the living God". God is, however, central to all the three groups, Orthodox, Conservative and Reform (though there are apparently a few Reform rabbis who are not certain about Him). The Reform case is that all shades of Jewish religious belief are a *halakhically*-acceptable option and part of *b'rit Sinai*. I don't think it is a valid argument.

The "words of the living God" text is in Eruvin 13b, which informs us, "For three years Bet Shammai and Bet Hillel were in dispute. One side said, 'The *halakhah* is in accordance with us'. The other said, 'The *halakhah* is in accordance with us'. A heavenly voice said, 'These, and these, are the words of the living God, but the *halakhah* is in accordance with Bet Hillel'."

The text admits that there can be several interpretations of a law but insists that in behavioural matters there is no room for indecision. It does not approve *halakhic*/non-*halakhic* pluralism because both Bet Hillel and Bet Shammai are within the *halakhic* loop. Not that one is inside the *halakhah* and one outside it. Both accept the authority of the *halakhah*, each with a different *halakhic* style or nuance.

One cannot use this passage to say that *halakhah* and the abrogation of *halakhah* are both Judaism. It is like saying that *kosher* and non-*kosher* are both *kosher*. Neither Bet Hillel nor Bet Shammai can be used to lend support to this position.

12

PRAYING FOR THE RABBIS

The Shabbat service has two prayers for the community - *Yekum Purkan* ("May Deliverance Arise") in Aramaic and *Mi Sheberakh* in Hebrew. They are preceded by another *Yekum Purkan* which prays for the rabbis and sages.

Which rabbis and sages? Until the Baer *Siddur* in the 19th century, the prayer concerned itself with religious leaders in ancient Palestine and Babylon. Adding the rabbis of the whole Jewish world modernised the prayer and enhanced its significance.

The prayer began with the dedication of the Temple, "When Solomon had concluded praying all this prayer and supplication… he stood and blessed all the congregation of Israel with a loud voice" (I Kings 8:54).

There is little evidence of prayers for the sages until the 10th century CE, when Nathan HaBavli described the installation of the Babylonian exilarch, who was even mentioned in the *Kaddish*. Other sages whose names were added to the *Kaddish* were a 9th century Ga'on, and also Maimonides, whom the Yemenites mentioned in their *Kaddish* in his lifetime. In *Mahzor Vitry* (c. 1100 CE), the prayers for the congregation and the sages are combined.

Though probably composed in Babylonia – hence the Aramaic wording – the prayer for religious leaders is not found in this form in the Babylonian or Sephardi rites. The text resembles the *Kaddish D'Rabbanan*, originally recited after a rabbinical discourse. It mentions the sages of Palestine and Babylonia, the judges, teachers and students. Of course the scholars of Iraq

(Babylonia) and their traditions are now dispersed, whilst in Israel there has been a great resurgence of Torah learning and *gedolei ha-dor.*

Even when Palestinian and Babylonian Judaism were transplanted to other parts of the Jewish world, *Yekum Purkan* did not acknowledge the sages "in every land of the Dispersion" until the publication of the Singer *Siddur,* acting upon Baer's suggestion in *Avodat Yisra'el. Maḥzor Vitry* mentions the exilarch, the political leader of Babylonian Jewry, thus covering both religious and lay leadership. *Vitry* does not have the plural *reshei galuta,* as there was only one exilarch at a time. Perhaps the plural corresponded with the plurals used for other dignitaries. The term *chavurata kadishta* does not denote a burial society but the Palestinian Sanhedrin, especially in the *ga'onic* period whose members were called *chaverim.*

Why is the prayer omitted on festivals? Probably in order not to delay people's return home for their festival meals.

I would like to see every community praying for its leaders and every congregation praying for its rabbi. Rabbinical and lay leaders often have a thankless task.. The prayer book remembers them kindly; we should too.

13

"SIT DOWN THE LOT OF YOU!"

I had a president whose father was the <u>h</u>azzan of an East End synagogue where they spoke more Yiddish than English. At that Shule the meetings were always rowdy, and the chairman had to shout to be heard. Once it got too much for him and he screamed out, *"Bleggages! Ob ir vill nicht up-shutten vill ich ois-chucken the whole b... y lot!"* It took me less than a minute to work out what he was saying; you might need a minute and a half.

Some of my Sydney congregants probably still remember the Rosh HaShanah when I shouted and "did my block" at the Great Synagogue during the *Musaf* service. I actually only lose my temper about once in two years, and that happened to be the occasion. Fortunately I didn't call anyone a *bleggage* - but I did shout, "Sit down! Be quiet!" The congregation were so shocked that the Shule was ghostly quiet for the rest of the service.

In some places the path to decorum is that the *gabbai* bangs hard on the reading desk and if necessary calls out, *"Sha! Sha!"*... maybe even *"Shah zoll zein!"* Of course he is calling for quiet, not for the return of the Iranian monarchy. Other *gabba'im* say *"Shtill!"* Or if they combine English and Yiddish, *"Mach a quietness!"* – or even *"Shurrup zoll zein!"*

In my first year in England I did a Shule-crawl in Golders Green on Simchat Torah and came into a <u>H</u>assidic *shtiebel* where the rabbi and congregants were having a shouting match. That little rabbi was vertically challenged and you could hardly see his head above his *shtender* - but when it got too much for him he rose to his full non-height, banged his hand down hard and yelled at them, *"Ich bin der rebbe doh!* I'm the rabbi round here!"

Maybe that's the way to assert rabbinic authority, to shout, *"Ich bin der rebbe doh!"* My own congregations were known for their dignity and decorum, unlike certain noisy places where there is hardly any reason to have a *hazzan* since you can't possibly hear him. I don't know why, but in some Shules outside Israel the more orthodox they claim to be, the less notice they take of the prohibition of talking during the service.

What happens when the rabbi stands up to speak? In most places there is no point in trying to chat during the sermon because all the rabbi will do is to wait until people are quiet and eventually the talkers will get the point.

Chief Rabbi Israel Brodie once gently rebuked a Rosh HaShanah congregation like this, "I know you haven't seen each other for a year but maybe by this point in the service you'll have exchanged greetings and said all that is necessary and we can continue with the prayers". Have a quietness on the High Holydays, and may it be a calm, peaceful year!

14

TEN LOST TRIBES

The Ten Lost Tribes weren't misplaced but displaced. This was Assyrian policy – they moved conquered peoples from one part of their empire to another, making them so busy settling down that they were unlikely to rebel against their overlords. So when Assyria defeated the northern kingdom of Israel in 722 BCE, most of the inhabitants of the kingdom were transported elsewhere and replaced by heathen settlers (II Kings 15-18). In their place a mixed multitude was transported to the plains and mountains of Israel.

Many passages prophesy that the tribes will come back to the Holy Land, so their descendants must still exist. The Midrash says that some of the "lost" tribes are on the western side of the river Sambation, some on the opposite side and others near Antioch. Various writers and messianic pretenders thought they had found Israelite tribes in places as varied as North Arabia, India, Abyssinia, Afghanistan, Japan and even Eastern Europe and South America. Those who favour the Indian theory think the ten tribes were the original Hindus and Buddhists. Adherents of the Eastern European theory insist that since the ten tribes were the Karaites whose ancestors had been in the Crimea since the 7th century BCE they could not, unlike Jews who suffered from Christian antisemitism, be blamed for the death of Jesus.

All sorts of people consider themselves Children of Israel, and pseudo-scholarship has worked out that almost every human group has a link to the ten tribes. This kind of "scholarship" even asserts that the word

"British" is really a combination of two Hebrew words – *b'rit* (covenant) and *ish* (man).

Wherever you live, there is likely to be a sizeable number of people with Jewish ancestry. Some re-claim their Jewish identity after centuries of estrangement. I know from my years on the Sydney Beth Din that people whose families came adrift from Judaism 200 years ago sometimes want to return to the fold. In some cases the original Jewish ancestor was sent to the Antipodes as a convict but then married a gentile and the children and later descendants lost their Jewish connection. There are also Jews like the founder of the Myer commercial empire, who willingly embraced the dominant faith and became part of the social establishment.

Normative Jews are unlikely to claim descent from the Lost Ten Tribes. The tribes transported by the Assyrians have long since merged into their surroundings and are no longer identifiable. When there was discussion about the status of the Karaite sect, the British Chief Rabbi, Hermann Adler, said that he was less concerned with the Karaites than the "Don't-care-ites". Along those lines, I am concerned about real-time Jews who drift away from Jewish life and end up as a (possibly sizeable) lost Jewish tribe...

15

THE FINAL CIGARETTE

I grew up at a time when being grown-up meant being able to smoke. Maybe ten a day was average. Ten *a day*? If I have smoked ten in my whole life, that's a lot. Smoking is bad for you, but at that stage few *halakhists* were saying such things. Many were heavy smokers themselves; on Shabbat they gasped for the three stars that marked the onset of nightfall.

My last cigarette was at a wedding reception where, to be part of the scene, I took a cigarette. Then the red-coated toastmaster proclaimed, "My Lords, bride and groom, ladies and gentlemen" (he then took out a *kippah* with a flourish and put it on his head), "pray silence for Rabbi Apple, who will recite Grace." Out went my cigarette and I never indulged again.

Another smoking memory is from a few years earlier, also in London. Not yet married, I was spending Shavu'ot in Stamford Hill with Marian's family. I spoke at the all-night *Tikkun* organised by Torah VaAvodah, an adult version of B'nei Akiva. I don't remember what I spoke about (no-one else does either), but someone gave me a cigarette which escorted me through the dark North London streets on the walk home. *Tikkun Leil Shavu'ot* – staying up on Shavu'ot to study Torah – is thus associated in my mind with smoking. The only logical connection is that Mount Sinai was wreathed in smoke when the Lord proclaimed the commandments.

There are of course more important reasons to study on Shavu'ot night. The Zohar declares that God and the People of Israel spend the night in conversation with each other. Others say that on the eve of the Giving of the Torah the Israelites slept so soundly that they had to be woken up for the Revelation, and later generations stay awake in order to atone for their lapse.

The Kabbalists quoted the "early men of piety" who spent that night in Torah study, saying, "Come, let's acquire the holy heritage for ourselves and our children in both worlds". Some quote the Mishnah that on Shavu'ot the fruit crops are judged. As there are people who remain awake on the night of Yom Kippur when man is judged, and some on Hoshana Rabbah, when the world is judged for rain, so we remain awake on Shavu'ot, anxious for the success of our crops. So the *Tikkun* of Shavu'ot has important antecedents, but it doesn't have to go with smoking.

We once had a chain-smoking bookkeeper in the Great Synagogue office in Sydney. The dense fog he caused in the office never seemed to bother him, but it annoyed the rest of us no end. Me, I would take the daily or Jewish paper and walk through the office vigorously fanning myself and trying to expel the smoke, but I'm not sure I achieved much. Eventually we got a new bookkeeper, but for other reasons.

16

TREES AND THE CRITICS

My childhood was made exciting by being able to plant trees in Israel. What a stroke of genius on the part of JNF to give ordinary people all over the world the opportunity to be part of up-building the land of Israel by purchasing a tree for such a modest sum that anyone could afford it.

Like everyone else, the first time I came to Israel I went looking for my tree. Then I realised that we were all in this together and the millions of trees we paid for as individuals were encompassed by vast forests and areas of greenery that made the whole of Israel flourish. These days, when I see a JNF forest I know that I am one of millions of little people who are part of countless big projects, and we are all part-owners of trees all over Israel.

I am especially proud that the Great Synagogue in Sydney, where I spent most of my rabbinical career, was the first congregation in Australia to sponsor a JNF forest in Israel, two in fact, and whilst I can't identify my tree or trees, I can certainly find the Great Synagogue forests on the map, and I have pictures of me present at the dedication of them both..

A second feature of my childhood was the communal critics. Those of us who were orthodox or on the way there, were bombarded by accusations that orthodoxy was hidebound, obscurantist, antiquated, unwilling to live in the real world. The world was making progress on every front, so we were told, and traditional Judaism was turning the clock back and anti-progressive.

If only the critics realised that so many of the popular occasions that gave them so much pleasure, like Tu BiSh'vat, the New Year for Trees, were developed by that same orthodoxy that they attacked, that same orthodoxy that had moulded constant growth within *halakhic* Judaism.

Tu BiSh'vat is part of the progressive record of orthodox Judaism. So is Simhat Torah, the popularity of which no-one can dare deny. Plus Bar- and Bat-Mitzvah. And solemn observances such as Yizkor and Yahrzeit. The criticisms are trite because they are so predictable, conventional and ill-informed.

There could never have been a JNF, nor could trees have become a world-wide Jewish contribution to Zionism and Israel, without a Jewish orthodoxy that created a Tu BiSh'vat and established it in the Jewish calendar.

The trite critics are so mean and unfair when they fail to acknowledge the power and grandeur of the orthodox tradition.

Since those early days of my Melbourne childhood I have been working on the trite critics. They owe me and others of my ilk an apology, and a vote of thanks.

17

RABBIS WHO LACK THE SPIRIT

I heard someone say, "I don't think my rabbi is really very spiritual". Since others complain that their rabbis don't give a lead, maybe we have a paradox – spiritual leaders who are neither spiritual nor leaders.

Both aspects need analysis: first, the word "leaders". There are rabbis who hold key positions in a range of organisations, who formulate policy and achieve changes, and think they are the kings of the community. Other rabbis are quieter and gentler, play no public role but have an aura and influence; they are revered for their thoughts, example, wisdom and counsel.

Leadership can function in the public arena; it can work behind the scenes. Moses asked God to replace him with a leader who would go out before the people and come in before them, a shepherd to guide the flock. He was granted a public-arena successor, Joshua, a man "in whom was spirit". Other leaders have a different kind of spirit and (another Biblical phrase) their soul is bound up with their people's soul.

Some rabbis are basically functionaries who do life-cycle events, operate synagogue mechanisms and leave the ideas to others. They are necessary but can't be called leaders. A few others say a rabbi can be an atheist and that "God" in the *siddur* is to be read figuratively. These are in the wrong profession. What about the rabbis who have prayed all their life but are still not certain who they are praying to? I won't name names, but I could. So can their congregants: Shule-goers are not always so *frum*, but they're not stupid. A certain lady told me, "Our rabbi loves the limelight, but he'd rather that God didn't share it with him"; I thought she had hit the nail on the head.

Some rabbis may really be pious and spiritual but they have a narrow Judaism, making a fuss about the length of your sleeves, how fast you can *shockle*, or whether your cellphone is kosher. They tell you it's part of God's pattern; others think they can't see the wood for the trees. Many of our Jews have no patience for what they deem minutiae, but they yearn for spiritual elevation and even turn to eastern religions to find it. When, as Rav Kook put it, the world is battered by wild catastrophes, we understand why sensitive souls "feel welling up within them a burning thirst for that inner substance and vision which transcends the discernible surface of existence". We let them down if they have no idea whether Judaism is capable of satisfying their spiritual seeking.

If the rabbi, the presumed repository of the wisdom of the ages and sages, cannot seem to personify the spiritual needs of the community, we have a bigger problem that we know. Maybe we should do away with the rabbi – or at least re-invent him.

18

PONDERINGS OF A PREACHER

My first sermon was actually long before my first ministerial appoinment in Bayswater. I pioneered distance education for the Jewish Education Board in Melbourne and had pupils in Tasmania. Hobart invited me to officiate on the High Holydays. On Rosh HaShanah I became a cantor and preacher. My cantorial skills were limited, though a predecessor had marked the Synagogue's big *Mahzor*, "Sing softly... Sing loudly". I had more potential as a preacher, though my first attempt in Hobart was a disaster. No-one had warned me how hard the Shule seats were and that people stood up and sat down during sermons. I read their actions as a sign of disapproval and brought the sermon to an unceremonious conclusion.

I was trained in homiletics and elocution at Jews' College. Mr. Johnson, the non-Jewish elocution teacher, attended my induction at Bayswater, thought I did a reasonable job and wrote to say so. The homiletics teacher, Rabbi Dr. Simon Lehrman, said that a good sermon was like his initials: SML – sincerity, modesty and learning. I spent an occasional Shabbat at Lehrman's Shule in North London. When he asked how I described his preaching, I had a brainwave and said, "Amplified conversation".

Dr. Lehrman (like my childhood rabbi, Jacob Danglow) did not fulminate or pontificate, and I guess I followed this pattern throughout my pulpit career. When a certain young man at the Great Synagogue said to his father, "I think the rabbi was speaking to me", the father passed on the comment and I took it as a great compliment. I thought of it when I saw a video of Rabbi Ephraim Mirvis' recent installation sermon as chief rabbi of Britain and I remarked to my wife, "He was good! He was talking to me!"

In London I heard the great Christian preachers but I decided that their theatrics weren't for me. My style was to try to talk to and with the people – relatively easy on Shabbat, when the attendance was smaller and I knew more or less everyone, harder on High Holydays, when the building was crammed from end to end. Even so, a lengthy incumbency made me comfortable with the congregation, and only once did I shout at them.

Another preacher from my youth, Rabbi Sholem Gutnick of Caulfield, told me that every sermon had to be Jewish. It had to utilise Jewish sources, notably the Midrash. I made sure that every sermon was a Jew speaking to Jews, though at the same time I was an Australian speaking to Australians (and prior to this, at Bayswater and Hampstead, a Brit speaking to Brits).

These days I rarely preach, though sometimes I give a *D'var Torah* in Hebrew. I watch Chief Rabbi Yisrael Lau on Israeli TV and he's really good. Some others are inaudible, and it's possibly better that way.

19

HOW MUCH ARE YOU WORTH?

In ancient Israel one could donate to the sanctuary the sum of money which represented the valuation a person placed upon himself or one of the family. It was a technical procedure. The amount of the valuation ranged from five to 50 shekels depending on whether you were male or female, young or old. The criterion was social usefulness – your worth to the community.

Had the question been about the value of a person's body, the answer would have been unimpressive. It was estimated in pre-decimal days that a man weighing 140 pounds contained enough fat for seven cakes of soap, carbon for 9000 pencils, phosphorus for 2200 match heads, magnesium for one dose of salts, iron to make one medium-sized nail, lime to whitewash a chicken coop, sulphur to rid one dog of fleas, and water to fill a 10-gallon barrel.

Shakespeare, on the other hand, said, "What a piece of work is a man! How noble in reason! How infinite in faculties! In form and moving how express and admirable! In action how like an angel! In apprehension how like a god! The beauty of the world! The paragon of animals!" To him a person's value was too high to be assessed in dollars and cents.

What *we* do is to judge a person by where they live, what car they drive, what they have, even how they dress. A Shule president I knew used to say, "Yes, we'll give that man an Aliyah. His suit looks tidy enough!" No: real worth depends on character, integrity, humanity, personality, and the

Divine spark in one's being. There is no way one person can be measured against another. Each is unique. None is a carbon copy or clone.

One of the banes of my life was the question that always followed the High Holydays: "How many people were at your Shule?" I more or less knew the answer, but I was reluctant to tell. I would have reduced everyone to a number, a cog in a wheel, a crowd of indistinguishable grey faces. When I spoke, I was addressing separate individuals with their own personal mix of talents, capacities and blessings. Each had their own personality, their own problems, their own promise. True, they made up a crowd, and the crowd had a personality of its own because of the shared moment. The moment the rabbi loses sight of the infinite distinctiveness of each individual he turns human beings into what an Australian politician called a population stamped out on cookie cutters.

What are you worth? The answer is unrelated to bank accounts or investments. It depends on your individual make-up and the way you assess what you can do for society, whether a five- or fifty-dollar contribution.

20

BOILS AND PROSELYTES

Does the Talmud really compare converts to boils? The saying, in Yev. 47b, possibly reflects the negative view in an ancient debate. A positive view is found in sources which praise those who bring gentiles "under the wings of the Divine Presence". The Midrash says that the Holy One, blessed be He, yearns for the nations to come to Him. The Tanḥuma says, "Dearer to God is the proselyte who has come of his own accord than all the crowds of Israelites who stood at Mount Sinai". The messianic prophets dream of all the nations coming to the Mountain of the House of the Lord.

The passage about boils is a play on words based on Isa. 14:1 which says that "the stranger shall join himself – *v'nisp'ḥu* - with them (the people of Israel) and cleave to the House of Jacob". The sages link *v'nisp'ḥu* with *sapaḥat*, a skin disease. Explanations include the following:

- Proselytes often observe Jewish law better than born Jews.
- A *sapaḥat* can be harmful but it can also be healing and beneficial.
- Sometimes a proselyte lapses and goes back to his/her previous ways.
- Some "converts" have an ulterior motive.
- The proselyte lacks Jewish lineage.

I know of people who try to enter the Jewish community in order to do missionary work from within, which is ethically, intellectually and spiritually dishonest. George Foot Moore says in his 3-volume book, "In the persecution under Hadrian (proselytes) were under strong temptation to clear their own skirts by turning informers". Yet the *Talmudic Encyclopedia* is unambiguous: "It is an obligation for a Bet Din to accept a gentile who comes to be converted, and to convert him according to Jewish law".

I spent many years as a Beth Din member and was involved in countless interviews with applicants for conversion as well as the ceremony of acceptance of successful candidates. In Israel both Marian and I taught in the Rabbinical Council of America's conversion classes. I always feared that some people who were accepted into Judaism might prove to be less than full-throated members of the Jewish people. There were a few converts who let me down, and I worry about their consciences.

But subject to adequate safeguards I still feel that making more proselytes would be good for the individuals concerned, good for the Jewish people, and good for the world. Individuals need the Jewish pattern of beliefs and practices as a source of spiritual certainty and inspiration. The Jewish people needs more strength, including the strength that comes from numbers. The world needs the stability and good sense of the Jewish idea.

21

WHY DOES A JEW LAUGH?

With so many problems, why do we Jews still laugh so much? Not only as individuals but as a people. There are even set times for humour in the Jewish calendar - especially Purim, the quintessential Jewish carnival.

We laugh at all our enemies, even the Nazis *yimmah shemam*. We laugh at the fate which our enemies planned. We didn't simply sit and weep, even shout – nor, for that matter, merely pray, though we would have accepted any miracle which God would have sent to save us. We knew we'd outlived all our foes, and were amused that latter-day enemies thought they would succeed where nobody else had.

- We laugh at our situation, not liking it one bit but seeing the funny side and thinking – and grateful - that somehow it wasn't even worse.
- We laugh at how complex we are – a religion but also a people, a people but also a religion, a nation with a land where only half of us live, a combination of several cultures at one and the same time...
- We laugh at how strange we are to the gentiles: our faith and ethics are the basis of their own civilisation, yet they accuse us of failing to see the light; our land is tinier than almost any other, yet our state hits more headlines than anywhere else except the USA and Russia.

- We laugh at how terrible the United Nations thinks we are, whilst it forgets the real *reshai'm* that break all the laws of human rights.
- We laugh because everyone thinks we are a monopolistic people wishing to control the world - but we can't control ourselves, rarely agree with one another and our internal squabbles use all the bad words we can import from other peoples' curse-language.
- We laugh because we deserve a better deal.
- We laugh because otherwise we would have to cry...

I always found public life serious and stressful. Handling difficult people and trying to get them on side, diffusing tense situations, putting out fires, looking for the right word, the right gesture, the right tone of voice – nothing ever came easily. Often I kept a poker face whilst inwardly seething.

What saved my sanity (presuming that I did emerge relatively sane)? I saw the funny side of a situation, though I would never have admitted it. I laughed at myself and indulged in some healthy self-deprecation.

Why did I tell such bad jokes? It's not that I wanted to be a comedian, but it's a way of letting off steam. Rev. William Katz once said to me (at a funeral!), "You'll have a hard job to keep this community sane!" If I preserved my own sanity that's already something.

22

GOD'S RELIGION

How can God have a religion? Whom could He worship? Our ancestors pondered this question and said that one can argue that God talks to Himself. He says when He looks at his world and His creations, "May My mercy outweigh My judgment!" In a poetic sense He even acts like a pious Jew and puts on *tallit* and *tefillin*. As human *tefillin* praise the oneness of God, so the Divine *tefillin* praise the uniqueness of the people of Israel.

This doesn't mean to say that Israel are always paragons of virtue, but they do their best. God appreciates the pain and pressure under which they try to uphold their faith. In the covenant relationship between Creator and created, each party yearns for the approval of the other. It is probably unique to Judaism to imagine that God wonders, "Am I acting too strictly?", and engages in self-scrutiny. In that sense one could say He has a religion, but looked at objectively, human attributes and actions attributed to Him are poetry which must not be taken too literally.

I offer these remarks because of all the questions that people ask, God is – rightly - at the top of the list. I found the questions rather predictable after a few years. "Rabbi, I know I don't come to Shule so often, but I'm still a good person, aren't I?" "Rabbi, isn't religion about what goes on in your head and heart, not what you eat and drink?" "Rabbi, Friday night is a wonderful idea, but why can't I switch on and off the electric lights on Shabbat?" To these and similar questions I worked out my answers and hoped that people were relatively satisfied. On occasions I laced the answer with some mild humour, but not everybody likes that approach. For them the query is highly serious, the result of thought and conscience, and the last thing the rabbi should do is to seem to be belittling the questioner.

The questions about God tend to address either His existence or the way He runs the world. Sometimes the question arose out of the Holocaust, sometimes from personal circumstances ("Why did God take my baby? Why did God let me down? Why didn't He let my grandmother live a bit longer?"). Belief in God was always hard. Our relationship with God was never easy. We knew He worked with wisdom but He was often too wise for limited human minds to understand. Why didn't we unilaterally abrogate our covenant with Him? Because life without God was unthinkable. To be left bereft in a hard, cold, rudderless world was no answer to anything.

23

NOTES IN THE WALL

In Jerusalem every day - and any day - is both yesterday and today. Street names evoke ages as disparate as King David and King George. The buildings are a jumble of the Bible, the Koran, the 19th century European Christian missionaries, and the Champs Elysees. The people are mystics and moderns, sometimes rolled into one: believers who move sedately, lost in meditation; pietists who scurry in search of a chance to study or to pray; old women who lug their heavy shopping trolleys, students with back-packs on the way to a lecture, youngsters in skimpy dress who meet their friends in an underground disco or bar. Jerusalem belongs to them all.

Jerusalem is an elevated site, where life is always on a high. There are stairs, and walls. The wall *par excellence* is the *Kotel Ma'aravi*, the Temple's Western Wall that has survived generations of conquerors. What happens at that Wall depends on who you are. It is customary to place a little scrap of paper in the Wall's crevices. Popes and presidents, politicians, priests and poets; athletes, actors and artists; people of all creeds, colours and cultures - all leave their prayers.

The little scraps are *k'vitlach* or *tzettlach,* in Hebrew *pitka'ot.* They are not so much written with ink as with tears. It doesn't matter if once in a while the notes are collected and given reverent burial. The message has been heeded; whatever the answer, the person concerned already feels better. What the messages are about is health, happiness, serenity, success, good marriages, good children, family stability... and world peace.

In the 18th century Rabbi Hayyim ibn Attar of Morocco learnt that his disciple, Hayyim Yosef David Azulai, was planning to live in Israel, and he asked him to place a letter in the Wall. Others say that when Attar gave a note to a poor man who needed help, the recipient meant to place it in a crack of the wall but the wind blew it away. Someone read it and was able to help him. So 300 years ago there were already notes in the wall.

The prayers in the crevices all ask for Divine support and intervention. Rav Kook says, "A person should train himself not to rely on God's Providence other than for things which humans cannot do themselves". Place *k'vitlach* in the wall by all means, but don't expect God to do all the work. Ask Him for things you are unable to do on your own. Ask Him for the wisdom and strength to use every ounce of ability to do His will.

I like to stand in a quiet corner near the Wall and think about what I could achieve if only I utilised whatever abilities God has given me. I try to do what Isaiah calls *ze'er sham, ze'er sham* – "a little here, a little there".

24

BURNING THE BOOKS

The Tisha B'Av dirges include a 13th-century poem by Me'ir of Rothenburg, "*Sha'ali S'rufah BaEsh* – Ask, you who have been burnt by fire". The poem does not weep for the Temple or even for the martyrs who died for God's Name. It is simply concerned with the burning of books.

Our tradition always regarded books as living beings, treated with respect, given honoured burial when their life came to an end. Why think of burnt books when there were so many burnt bodies? Because the books our enemies destroyed were themselves martyrs. So were their authors, because when human life is cheap, no-one wants to save authors or artists.

On 17 June, 1242, the mobs – incited by an apostate Jew and endorsed by the pope and the king of France – threw 24 cartloads of Hebrew manuscripts onto the flames in a Paris square, symbolic of seven centuries of holocausts of Jewish books that extended to the Nazi destruction of at least three million Jewish books. In a cold, hostile world, books were often our only friends, and destroying them was an attack on Judaism. Our books represented independent thinking and defiance. They were a threat to the a-morality in which nothing was sacred – values, conscience, life itself.

In Roman times Rabbi Hananya ben Teradyon was wrapped in the Torah scroll from which he had been teaching, and thrown onto the flames. His pupils, unable to save him, called, "Master, what do you see?" His answer: "Burning parchments, but letters flying upwards!" Enemies destroyed the parchments, but the message of the books could not be destroyed.

I thought of the book burnings when I met Holocaust survivors. Outside Israel, Australia took in more survivors than any other country. When I addressed the Shabbat service at the Survivors' Gathering in Sydney in the 80s, I wept with the survivors - and laughed too, because they had the last laugh, not Hitler (cursed be his name). I thought of the book burnings, when one of my Hampstead congregants, Michael Zylberberg, asked me to translate the verse he had selected as the dedication for his *Warsaw Diary*. I thought of the book burnings when another congregant told me, "I am a *gilgul*. I escaped from Auschwitz". *Gilgul* means transmigration of a soul, or reincarnation. Gershom Scholem writes, "Its singular purpose was always the purification of the soul and the opportunity to improve its deeds".

When I apply to modern Jewry the phrase, "Burning parchments, but letters flying upwards", I weep for the parchments but rejoice for the letters. The world tells us to forgive and forget; it wonders why we don't lie down and die. Who says we have to listen? We were dead but now we are alive.

25

RABBIS DON'T KNOW IT ALL

How can we square Jewish tradition, which says the world is 5774 years old, with the scientific view that posits a vastly longer period? The problem was recognized in *Tanakh* itself, especially in Psalms, and widely debated in the *Midrash*. Medieval thinkers of course addressed it in a sophisticated way.

The crucial issue is how to interpret the seven *days* of creation - listed in Genesis 1-2. Do we read them literally or allegorically? If literally, we have seven times 24 hours and a relatively short period of history – millennia and not eons - thereafter. If allegorically, learning from Psalm 90:4 that "day" can be a thousand years, then Genesis 1-4 becomes a long, majestic poem of beginnings. In that case, the expressions of time need not be taken literally and Genesis 1-2 is not a scientific analysis but (to use Aboriginal-type language) a "narrative of the dreamtime". But problems remain, e.g.

- The material is not mathematically verifiable, since mathematics was not yet developed.
- When did time begin? The Creation story happened before the science of time, though it was recorded in an age of time.
- If we can treat the "Creation" parts of the *Tanakh* allegorically we must distinguish between poetical (*Aggadah*)and legal texts (*Halakhah*), and insist that *halakhic* material not be allegorized.

Whatever the age of the world, the really important verse is "In the beginning, God created" (Gen. 1:1). There is a God, a creating God, whose wish for His world is that His creatures should live by His moral law.

The problems are harder than for Maimonides because science had not reached the point it has today. Because Maimonides was scientist as well as rabbi, he could discuss the problems as an expert. Some writers ask whether it was faith or reason which was uppermost in his mind; Isidore Epstein proved that for all his philosophy, Maimonides' final arbiter was faith.

I have no pretensions to scientific authority, nor do I compare myself to the Rambam. True, as a high school student I achieved a 100% mark in mathematics, but I never pursued the subject, though my rabbinical predecessor, Israel Porush, had a doctorate in mathematics. The most I could do, which embodies the advice I always gave to my colleagues, was not to presume that I had scientific training. When there was Jewish writing on the subject I brought it to the attention of the questioner. Otherwise I said, "For science, go to a scientist". What the rabbi offers is religion, the theological and ethical principles which suggest how to handle the scientific material.

26

TO 120!

Jews wish each other "To 120!" because the Torah says that Moses lived to 120 in good mental and physical shape. We wish a person to be like Moses. We hope they too will have a long life and retain their faculties.

Once upon a time the idea of living to 120 was unthinkable (though early Biblical forebears were said to have reached 900 or so). Life expectancy was lower. It was a real achievement – certainly a blessing – to reach 50 or 60. Old age homes took applicants from the age of 60, whilst now the average age is 80+. While some people in their 90s say when they enter the Montefiore Home in Sydney, "Why did I leave it so long?", one such person who felt he was too young used to go walkabout and find his way back to the suburb he came from.

Some old people have mental clarity and a declining body: others are in the opposite situation. The ideal is a body that remains in good condition and a mind that remains sharp. Moses was fortunate because "his eye was not dim nor his natural force abated" (Deut. 34:7). How then could he complain (Deut. 31:2), "I am no longer able to go out and come in"? The rabbis say, "He would have been able to go about as before, but God would not allow it" – i.e., his life span was reaching its end and his active career was over.

These days there are facetious modifications of the traditional wish, such as "May you live to 120 and six months". Why an extra six months? "You wouldn't want to die suddenly, would you?" Another version: "May you live to 125". Why an extra five years? "To allow for inflation!" Me, I don't have the old energy and resilience. I used to be on the go from early morning onwards and could fit in several evening engagements too. Some Sundays I would give seven speeches in one day, generally all in different locales, and even so would find myself criticised for failing to put in an appearance at one or two additional community functions.

A major problem in all my congregations was how to increase the Shule attendance. I urged the seniors to get up, get dressed and get out every Shabbat and come to Shule. Not only would it fill the time and bring them warmth and fellowship, but it would be a great support for the Synagogue. It would give younger people the chance to see what a talented group of people made up the congregation. So many had been through amazing experiences and indeed adventures and it is a pity that they didn't all take the opportunity to record their life story. I learnt this myself when I began to seek background information about my family and regretted that I had been too impatient in my youth to listen more seriously to my parents.

27

WHAT IBN EZRA MEANS TO SAY

When I was a student in London, Dr. Naphtali Wieder lectured on Bible Commentary. He used to ask rather rhetorically, not "What does Ibn Ezra say?" but "What does Ibn Ezra *mean to say*?" We had to look behind the words of the commentator to find the point he was trying to make. Dr. Wieder was not only teaching exegesis but giving us a sound principle of judgment, which I for one have used throughout my life. When people said (or wrote) things, I instinctively asked, "What are they *really* saying?" In the world of academic scholarship Dr. Wieder's principle often stood me in good stead. All writers were subjected in my mind's eye to the Wieder test.

Rabbi Kopel Kahana had a similar approach when it came to Talmud and Jewish law codes. His question was, "What do we have on the operating table?" To train us in legal reasoning, Rabbi Kahana wanted us to recognise the real point at issue and not be diverted elsewhere by side issues. The Kahana test, like the Wieder test, became one of my constant tenets.

I have often applied both tests to the way the world has come to treat Israel. When the "settlements are illegal in international law" mantra began, someone I know had a routine retort, "Settlements, schmettlements – they didn't like us before the settlements were thought of, and they still don't!"

After World War II there was a honeymoon with the Jews. Sensitive Christians felt bad about the Holocaust and saw what had been caused by careless and anti-historical Christian teaching about Judaism. People who felt the Jews deserved a fair go saluted the establishment and survival of the Jewish State. The Six-Day War left them amazed and admiring.

Then the maligning and misrepresentation of Israel started in earnest. At times they had the decency to pay lip service to Israel's achievements – "Israel is a tough little democracy, *but...*" What were they really saying? "We are giving you the benefit of political correctness, but we wish Israel and the Jews would go away". Then the lip service was dropped and they bluntly enumerated Israel's sins and blithely waved aside its virtues.

You might have thought that the Wieder and Kahana tests were irrelevant and the world was now saying what it meant: "The Jews are a nuisance and always were. Christianity tried to get rid of them and gave them centuries of suffering. Hitler tried to get rid of them and destroyed millions. We use different weapons – especially words – and we will be the ones to succeed".

They try this game on the university campuses and the international arenas, but there is no way they will win. Not only can and will we defend ourselves, but without us their life-blood and civilisation will only dry up and disappear.

28

APPLE AND HONEY

Sydney had a Rabbi Apple, Melbourne a Rabbi Honig. Jointly we symbolised a sweet new year marked by apple dipped in honey. Why my name is Apple is explained in my book, "To Be Continued". The name Honig may have come from the early days of Jewish surnames in Europe, when Jews who were on good terms with the regime, or could pay a good bribe, got nice names. The history of apples is said to go back to the Garden of Eden, but Genesis only mentions fruit in general. What Eve gave Adam to eat may have been an *etrog*. Apples figure in many verses of *Shir HaShirim* as a source of health. Not only are they good for you but they have a good taste and aroma, and the apple tree provides shade.

In the Bible honey was from dates (or possibly grapes: Rashi says on Lev. 2:11 that *devash*, "honey", is the sweet juice of any fruit). The manna the people ate could have tasted like cake and honey. By Philistine times, honey was mostly from bees, as we see from Samson's riddle, "What is sweeter than honey?" (Judges 14:14, 18). No-one questioned the *kashrut* status of apples, but they had a *halakhic* problem with honey, since bees are not kosher. The rule is that whatever comes from an unclean animal is unclean, for example the milk of pigs. The sages, however, rule that honey is *kosher* because the bee merely stores it (Bekhorot 7b).

Australian rabbis had surnames from many sources. Some are from first names such as Abraham, Jacob, Solomon, Boas and Myer. Some are from place names: examples are Brodie and Gurewicz; Rapaport is from "Rav Oporto". There are abbreviations, e.g. Katz (*Kohen Tzedek*) and

Brasch (*Ben Rabbi Shimon*). There are "valuable" names like Goldman and Silberman, and possibly Blumenthal and Freedman. Animal names figure – especially Wolf. Professions play a part in names such as Belfer ("teacher's helper"), Singer and Kantor. Australia does not seem to have had spiritual leaders with their rabbinical status articulated in names such as Rabbinowitz.

The important thing about rabbis is not their names but their contribution. Once Australia was a small, distant, almost irrelevant outpost, but even then its rabbis would have been an ornament anywhere, and there were strongly Jewish families for whom Jewish tradition was highly prized. Today it is the 9th largest Jewish community, with a constantly growing level of Jewish education and observance. Rabbis are no longer mostly functionaries concerned with prayers, pastoral services and elementary Bible stories. No longer is it the characteristic picture, in the rabbinic phrase, that "more than the calf wishes to drink, the mother wishes to give milk". Now the calf increasingly wants to drink, and the quality of the rabbinate is impressive.

29

WAS EINSTEIN A RELIGIOUS MAN?

Many people who belong to congregations are not religious. What brings them to the synagogue on high days, holydays and life-cycle events is a feeling that that is where they ought to be – a vague idea to be sure, but it seems to do them some good, apart from the benefit to the synagogue of having seats on seats. Trying to work out what a really religious person would be, led me to think about some of our great Jews.

Rav Kook remarked to his doctor, "The day will come when those who are great Jews will be great as Jews". Let me ask whether another great Jew, Albert Einstein, was a religious man. Most people say "No". He wasn't a synagogue-goer. He kept few *mitzvot*. He rejected traditional God ideas. Yet he was a spiritual person obsessed with ultimate questions. Already as a child he believed in an energy behind events. He wrote that there were three stages in religion: *the exaltation of fear* (religion as a way of appeasing the forces that control external events), *a social* feeling whereby God "protects, disposes, rewards and punishes", and *a cosmic religious feeling* ("manifestations of the profoundest reason and the most radiant beauty").

This third category gave Einstein a spiritual quality. He did not have a personal God who loved and spoke to His creatures, evoking the loving response of obedience to the Divine will. He had a profound moral sense but did not proclaim that science alone cannot guide human conduct.

It's in the Einstein sense that many people are spiritual but not religious. Or am I wrong, and maybe they have a dimension that Einstein lacked? Don't they have a feeling of being in the presence of a Presence, some sort of relationship with God? What makes a moral instinct religious, however, is that God has commanded it, and I believe that most Jews have that feeling.

What would make me absolutely certain of people's religiosity would be if they chose to follow religious patterns and commandments. In some cases it will eventually come: the Talmudic rabbis said, *"mittokh shello lishmah ba lishmah* – from acting with an ulterior motive one comes to do the right thing for its own sake"*. But even if that stage never comes, no-one must be denigrated or dismissed. I heard someone say in the days when travel to the moon was a hypothetical futuristic dream, a complete Mission Impossible, "We mightn't reach the moon, but we will get further than the person who says it isn't even worth trying!" The mark of a religious person is that they are continually trying to reach God, and as Rav Kook said, even the search for God is in itself a religious quest.

30

WHO OWNS ME?

In ancient days people owned their slaves. Forget about slavery (though it is a major ethical problem) - who owns me? One view is that I own myself and have control over my own person. Justice Cardozo said, "Every human being of adult years and sound mind has a right to determine what shall be done with his own body". A former Australian State Coroner told me that in the last resort a body belongs to the State. In Judaism, my body does not belong to me, nor to the State, but to God: "The body is the property of the Holy One, blessed be He" (*Shulḥan Arukh HaRav*). Hence no-one may injure or mutilate their person or authorise anyone else to do so. Even after death, that would be an offence against God. Cremation is the ultimate destruction of the body. Only actions authorised by the Creator may be carried out on my person. A body may be healed but not destroyed.

Whilst I can't be certain that cremation is wrong for non-Jews, the basic attitude of Jewish ethics would be against it. Ancient body-burning was a pagan, barbaric act, and despite modern refinements in crematoria practices it remains pagan and barbaric. A patient I saw in hospital was an engineer whose professional specialty was designing bone-crushing machinery for crematoria. I said to myself, "Isn't Jewish burial more dignified, more emotionally satisfying? A body is respectfully prepared after death and reverently laid to rest in the earth. No-one deliberately crushes, burns and destroys it. What happens is up to God". Crushing and burning the physical remains should send shudders down the spine after the ghastly horrors perpetrated upon millions of human beings who were sent to the gas ovens. Cremation is crude and cruel whether the body is that of Jew or non-Jew. No-one, not even the State, has the right to offend God in this way.

I was often consulted by government, media and public bodies (forgive the *double entendre*) on social and ethical issues. Not only to do with death, but concerning life – abortion, the economy, education and so much more. My role at that point was not simply as a teacher of Judaism to Jews, but as a citizen speaking to fellow-citizens of every faith and none.

Could I impose the Jewish view on non-Jews? Clearly no, but neither could I abdicate and say, "Decide for yourselves". The rabbi was consulted because this is a laisser-faire generation. The world does not need to feel and think as we do, but it dare not say that anything goes and everything is up to individual opinion. I had great respect for Chief Rabbi Jakobovits, of whom it was said that he was Margaret Thatcher's Jewish Archbishop of Canterbury. His teachings were firmly orthodox, and Margaret Thatcher sensed that a nation needed firm moral guidance.

31

ANTISEMITISM - ENDEMIC OR EPIDEMIC

Antisemitism is alive again, often cloaked as criticism of Israel. Ask the antisemite about other nations that kill their own people, and you will hear, "Yes, but we don't like Jews!" Replace ignorance and bigotry with facts and fairness, and you'll eradicate prejudice. Start with *facts,* proving that Israel is far from an apartheid state, and showing how the whole world benefits from what we do in so many fields. Be *fair.* You don't have to like everything about Jews and Israel, but you don't need to destroy them.

Where did antisemitism begin? Not with human nature, nor Islam, nor the anti-Judaism of the ancient world, but with Christianity. Attacking it must begin with Christianity. Prelates tell Jews not to say that the scriptures justify Zionism, as if anyone can erase Zion from the Bible. Synods decide, despite the evidence, that Jews treat Palestinians without compassion.

High-minded Christians admit that condemning Israel and Judaism is not essential to Christian theology. But antisemitism derives from that theology. It argues that Jews should have died out or become Christians long ago. It is bothered that Jews have survived and created a State. It says, "There is no salvation outside the Church". It claims, "The Jews crucified Jesus" (they didn't!) – "so let's crucify the Jews!" It destroyed innumerable Jewish lives.

Prelates speak rhetorically about interfaith amity and loving one's neighbour, but I want to know why every branch of Christianity doesn't stand up boldly and speak out against the anti-Jewish calumnies. I want to know why Christian leaders don't take their tolerance to the streets and allow Jews – and everyone - the right to be themselves.

I want to know why they don't explain that Jesus was a Jew, not a Christian, who had no intention to create a new faith and would be quite at home in a synagogue. I want to know the logic of blaming the Jews for killing Jesus whilst arguing that his death removed sin from the world.

I want to know why, if God allows Jews and Judaism in His world, the Christians can't take a leaf out of His book: why Christians can't acknowledge human conscience and say that others have a right to be.

Once when a newspaper printed a letter from me, a reader asked where my Christian compassion was. A rabbi is not a Christian... but genuine Christians would show respect to the Judaism from which their Jesus came.

Jews always respond when Christians and Muslims are under attack. Christians and Muslims should reciprocate – even, indeed especially, those who criticise Israel. It would be good for Christian and Muslim self-respect. I believe in working with other faiths, but sometimes my patience is tested.

32

ENEMIES

When a Melbourne rabbi died, a columnist said rather nastily, "Rabbi ... made some enemies, but he is not the only rabbi with that gift". Actually the rabbi concerned was a people-person able to connect with human beings. He had enemies, but he had a legion of friends. I was amongst them. And there is a saying: "The person who never made an enemy never made anything"

I don't know how many friends I made, but I don't think I had many enemies. Yes, there were people with whom I disagreed, but I tried to avoid rancour and revenge, and generally we remained polite. If I made decisions which were not popular, there were lay leaders who complained that I was espousing positions which were bound to cause upset. Occasionally those to whom I looked for support made themselves scarce. But if my conscience required a certain stand, no matter how diplomatic I was, I had no choice.

Some people left the Shule and joined another, not always for the most honorable reasons. I felt personally hurt because sometimes they had been close to me and my family and had sat at our table. I did not like it when few had the decency (or courage) to be up-front and discuss the matter with me first, and it also hurt if they bad-mouthed the Shule they had left. It was little consolation when one such person told me, "It wasn't because of you!"

It impressed me when a Christian periodical took up a controversial line on an issue and said, in words I have never forgotten: "Of course we have our enemies, but they are not people. They are prejudice, superficiality and arrogance." I echo that approach. I have enemies, but the enemies are not humans. Prejudice, superficiality and arrogance are my enemies too, but that's only a beginning. My list amounts to a baker's dozen.

The enemies I add are three Is, injustice, inefficiency, and impropriety; three Ms, mendacity, mealy-mouthedness and meanness, and three D's, disdain, demonization, and distortion of the truth. Plus sheer stupidity. Total: 13. Maybe the worst is stupidity, when you act like a donkey - but why insult the donkeys? Ahad HaAm said, "I am careful in my choice of enemies" – but most times you don't choose your enemies: they choose you.

How does one cope with enemies? By shouting at them? No enemy vanishes like smoke when someone shouts at them. The Bible has a surprising piece of advice. When you see your enemy's animal groaning under its load, help the animal without worrying about your problems with the owner. Change the load even if the enemy does not always become your friend. Bit by bit, chop away at what is causing pain and aggravation. Bit by bit, rebuild the world and make it a nicer place. That's how I have tried to handle the problem. I'm still working at it.

33

GOING TO THE DOCTOR

Some religions tell you to keep away from doctors and leave it all to God. Judaism doesn't agree. Of course the ultimate decisions as to life and death are in the hands of the Almighty. The Torah says, "I am the Lord your Healer" (Ex. 15:26): a clear, unambiguous statement. But when the Torah says, "He shall surely heal" (Ex. 21:19), we learn two things – one, as the Talmud says, "The doctor is permitted (by God) to heal", i.e. the physician is God's agent, and two, no-one has a right to side-step the medical profession and leave everything to God and His miracles. Jewish writing has an abiding interest in the way the body works, the use of the earth's resources in mending and healing, the way the brain given by God can be harnessed to daily living – all are axiomatic in Judaism. I know the sages say at the end of Kiddushin that the best of doctors is destined for Gehinnom, but this is a warning to doctors not to become too high and mighty.

Before a Medical Shabbat at the Great Synagogue in 1978 I worked out that one in 16 Jewish families included a doctor. It might even be an under-estimate. Jews in the healing professions have made so many changes for the better in the human condition that I wonder how the antisemites think anyone can survive if they boycott everything that has a Jewish involvement.

Jewish engagement with medicine was constant. Dr. Maimonides was far in advance of his time and pioneered psychosomatic medicine. Non-doctors such as the Baal Shem Tov had an instinct for healing. Jewish communities always had nurses, midwives and hospitals that were of a higher standard than in general society. The patient, their family, friends and community, had to pull their weight by prayer, fasting, cleanliness, diet, exercise and lifestyle. Washing oneself had a religious dimension; after using the toilet one washed their hands and said a *b'rakhah*. My Sydney doctor told me the best medicine was a healthy life-style.

I said something in my book of memoirs about a certain Yom Kippur afternoon when I caused a stir at the Hampstead Synagogue by feeling so ill that they more or less had to ask the congregation, "Is there a doctor in the house?" Actually there was no shortage of doctors, and I ended up that evening having an emergency operation for appendicitis at the Central Middlesex Hospital. It was no pleasure apart from the fact that the Ne'ilah sermon I had prepared was now unused and I could give it the following year, meaning that I had less work to do in getting ready for the next High Holydays...

34

NOT JOINING A SYNAGOGUE

All my life I have been a Shule-goer. It's such an ingrained habit that if I'm on holiday and don't have a Shule to go to I feel terrible. I remember my predecessor, Rabbi Israel Porush, saying after he retired, "I must say I miss the pulpit". Now that I too am retired I understand what he meant, though I don't have any compulsion to get up and give speeches.

Long ago I discovered that many Jews don't belong to synagogues. If they need a rabbi or Shule they find one. If invited to a life-cycle event, they come out of politeness. If a rabbi speaks at a civic event or on TV, they are proud. If a friend says, "I passed your synagogue today – what a lovely building!" they nod in agreement. But formal membership of a synagogue? No way. Why? Apathy: "I can't be bothered!" Economics: "Things are tough: I can't afford it!" Ideology: "I don't believe in any God – why should I join a place of prayer and God-talk? It wouldn't be honest."

It's not hard to answer the first two arguments. The third is more difficult. Numbers of synagogue members – let me call them "insiders" - also have difficulties with belief. Some join a synagogue for extraneous reasons ("I do it for my wife's sake... The Shule meant so much to my parents... I like the rabbi..."). The "insiders" will hopefully work through their position and come to a – possibly uneasy – truce with God, even if He's a God they don't or can't believe in. But the ideological outsider?

Synagogues have three main aspects, *bet k'nesset* (community centre), *bet midrash* (house of study) and *bet t'fillah* (place of prayer). All are intertwined, but for the purpose of this piece let me separate them.

- In the *bet k'nesset* we meet as a people. We express our Jewish identity and culture. In community centres, people play sport, enjoy music, watch films, have a coffee – admirable, but not essentially Jewish. What we do in the *bet k'nesset* has a Jewish aura, a Jewish ethos.. even without prayer and theology.
- In the *bet midrash* we encounter the Jewish texts and engage with them. We can all be enriched by more Jewish knowledge, even those who have problems with the outlook of the material.
- Is it the *bet t'fillah* that is the problem? If there are issues with God, they have to be worked through. There are many places to engage with the problem – on the beach, among the trees, in the library. If I may quote the Psalms, you can "commune with your own heart upon your bed". Why not commune with your heart and mind *in the synagogue*?

35

OLYMPIC IDOLATRY

The Olympic Games host nation always gears up with an outpouring of hype, beginning with the Olympic torch. The torch originated under pagan auspices and revived in Germany amid paganism of a different and worse kind. But carrying it through so much territory and involving so many people creates a sense of excitement and it may be unfair to judge it too harshly. If there is a problem it is with the Olympics themselves.

Sport itself was part of Biblical history. The ancient Israelites were a hardy, energetic people, engaged in running, archery, ball-playing, dancing, swimming, weight-lifting and sling-shooting. After the Biblical age other sports arose, ranging from gladiatorial contests to juggling. The Talmud tells fathers to teach their children to swim. Tacitus, no admirer of Jews, observed that "the bodies of the Jews are sound and healthy, and hardy to bear burdens". Yet the official Jewish attitude to sport was reserved. Greek and Roman athletics went with immodesty (sportsmen played naked, and some tried to obliterate their circumcision), idolatry, frivolity and cruelty, including throwing people to the lions. The games contradicted Jewish standards of decency and morality. Josephus records Jewish antagonism towards Herod when the king established his own five-yearly games and called one of his daughters Olympia.

Sport has rhythm, gracefulness, bodily co-ordination and sheer zest. The sporting industry makes it a commercial commodity. Robert Boyle writes in "Sport – Mirror of of American Life", "Sport permeates any number of levels of contemporary society, and it touches upon and deeply influences such disparate elements as status, race relations, business life, automotive design, clothing styles, the concept of the hero, language, and ethical values". Gone is the sheer enjoyment and exhilaration of stretching one's limbs, developing bodily prowess and cultivating sportsmanship. Sport is now something to be exploited, part of business and politics.

The modern Olympics were inaugurated by Baron Pierre de Coubertin in 1896. He believed the games would foster international brotherhood and harmony. Germany was the scene of the two worst episodes – Berlin in 1936 and Munich in 1972, which brought international terrorism into the sports arena. Thereafter there has been a further series of Olympic scandals.

Rav Kook, who thought that sport would make the youth of Eretz Israel into "courageous sons of their nation" and that "the air of the world will become holy and pure", would have been shocked at the grubby commercialism of modern sport, with corruption, cut-throat rivalry, and spectatorism that does nothing for the personal fitness of the barrackers.

36

SIX QUESTIONS

Maimonides' 13 Principles come in the Siddur in two versions – a credo in which each line begins "I believe with perfect faith", and the hymn known as *Yigdal*. Neither is by Maimonides himself. The original text is in his Mishnah Commentary as a preface to chapter 10 of tractate Sanhedrin.

Solomon Schechter says Maimonides compiled his list as a response to the claims of Christianity, Islam and Karaism. Maimonides himself says he is enumerating the views which would assure a person of a place in heaven.

A different list comes in Tractate Shabbat 31a/b which teaches that six questions are asked of everyone at Heaven's gate: "When they bring a person to judgment they say to him, 'Were your dealings honest? Did you devote time to Torah? Did you engage in procreation? Did you look forward to salvation? Did you reason wisely? Did you deduce one thing from another?'" The six are deduced from Isa. 33:6, "There shall be faith in your times, strength, salvation, wisdom and knowledge". They are not necessarily measures of achievement but marks of commitment. One does not need to become a great scholar but must give time to Torah; one does not have to produce a set number of children but must promote procreation.

When I was asked for the main heads of Jewish belief I generally said that we believed in a series of values – honesty, study, family, optimism, rationality and sound thinking. I said all six were essential for a good Jew but needed to go with piety, *Yirat HaShem*. The crucial thing was not a formal credo but a good spiritual, mental and emotional attitude to life.

As Leo Baeck points out, dogmatics (obligatory beliefs) are not necessary in Judaism, though they are in Christianity, which had to identify the areas where it differed from Judaism. Judaism had and has a theology, but it is an ongoing process of thinking, not a cut-and-dried series of conclusions. It can accommodate both the rationalism of Maimonides and the emotionalism of Hassidism. Even though the God ideas of, say, Spinoza and Kaplan are unorthodox, this does not automatically make these thinkers into atheists.

A further comment needs to be made. Religions are not interchangeable. Though Judaism and Christianity have points in common, it is a myth, as Arthur A. Cohen argues, to claim that there is a Judeo-Christian tradition. Though Islam shares some teachings with the other two monotheistic faiths, it has its own pattern and priorities. Not only religions but philosophies have widely differing ways of thinking even when they use the same words such as freedom, democracy, peace and human rights. When a United States spokesperson calls on another nation to accept democracy, each nation has its own notion of what the word means.

37

CHECKING THE INGREDIENTS

I found a higher proportion of people keeping kosher in Britain than Australia. There are historical and sociological reasons. The outcome is that Jewish observance in Australia is more difficult and probably more expensive because of the small size of the market. The supervision of kosher foods became a major part of my activities in Sydney, not that I did much supervising myself, though I did my share, but I was heavily involved in the official *kashrut* agencies of the community.

When Rabbi Osher Abramson was Av Beth Din, I often accompanied him on *kashrut* inspections, applying *halakhic* principles to real situations. Two memories stand out – how he tested the skills of a *shohet*, and how he handled the special problems of kosher food in a hospital kitchen.

I could write a history of the NSW Kashrut Commission, which later assumed other names and faced other challenges. I often played a diplomat's role in these organisations, smoothing things over, handling disgruntled individuals, and uniting two rival bodies. At one point I moved into open warfare, heading a group who set up the Kosher Consumers' Association in an attempt to bring Pesach and other prices down.

There was an occasion when a university caterer bypassed the Beth Din and Kashrut Authority and produced a supposedly kosher function at which meat - presumably from a kosher source - was served with butter, in breach of the dietary laws which require milk and meat foods to be kept separate. When questioned by guests, the caterer blithely said they had Rabbi Apple's approval. In fact Rabbi Apple knew nothing about it. My rule was never to give personal supervision to anyone or anything when there was an official communal *kashrut* organisation. Rabbi Apple came out of the experience unscathed but highly incensed – both on his own behalf and in the interests of the observant Jews whose scruples had been dishonoured.

I constantly faced the question of why consumers need to look up a kosher products directory. It is not just a matter of communal discipline but common sense. Food technology is so complex that consumers (even retailers) can't be sure what a product contains. Also there are *kashrut* rules that non-experts don't always know, such as whether a small amount of a prohibited ingredient can be ignored. In an emergency or if there is no *kashrut* expert you may have to do your own checks, but don't take the list on the label as the last word. Modes of manufacture can be changed without notice. Sometimes an unacceptable ingredient is suddenly utilised. In Israel I sit quietly on the sidelines, though it is a shock when some people invent their own kosher labels and deceive the public.

38

NO CHICKEN ON SHABBAT?

Our friends and Shabbat guests are incredulous: "You don't eat meat on Shabbat? Not even chicken?" They admit that our non-*fleishig* soups are actually quite tasty, they even like our *pareve cholent*, but they still wonder if what we do is really *kosher*.

It's not just that Shabbat and chickens seem to go together, but there is a view in the Talmud that Shabbat cannot be enjoyed without meat, and this is the sticking-point. Though God's original plan for mankind was vegetarian and the manna in the wilderness was vegetarian, the Torah permits the eating of meat. It lists animals which may be eaten and how to slaughter them, and it makes animal sacrifice part of Temple worship. Most people cannot imagine living without meat. Meat eating gives a feeling of fullness and satisfaction, which is where the Talmudic assertion, "there is no *simḥah*... without meat" (*Pes.* 109a) comes in. There is a kabbalistic view that meat-eating elevates the animal. But what about non-kabbalists?

The Talmud says, "eat meat sparingly" (*Ḥullin* 84a); but this is not an argument against the *principle* of meat eating, only the quantity. *Pesaḥim* 109a tells us, "Our rabbis said, 'A person is obligated to make his children and household rejoice on a festival... With what does he make them rejoice? With wine... Rabbi Yehudah ben Batyra said, 'When the Temple stood there could be no rejoicing except with meat... but now that the Temple is no longer in existence, there is no rejoicing except with wine, as it is said, 'Wine gladdens the heart of man' (Psalm 104:15)". Hence meat is no longer essential to *simḥah*, and the rule is not about meat but wine. There certainly can be no *simḥah* if meat eating causes a feeling of distress.

Maimonides endorses meat eating on festivals "if one can afford it", implying a different menu if a person were poor or if it gave them pleasure. The *Shulḥan Arukh* says that those who fast every day would feel pain if they had to eat on Shabbat, so we could add that vegetarians would feel pain if they had to eat meat on Shabbat (*OH* 288:1-3).

What turned me against meat is the ethic of killing animals for food. As part of rabbinic studies I had to learn the *halakhah* of *sheḥitah*, and to watch the *shoḥet* at work. I appreciated (and of course still do) the way in which *sheḥitah* minimises animal pain, but I became increasingly uncomfortable about killing animals so that humans could have meat. It took time, but we were eventually able to make the house meat-free, and we haven't been *fleishig* for years. I still had to make spot checks of butcher shops, but we did not patronise any of them. The communal wits used to say, "Did you know that Rabbi Apple doesn't go to a kosher butcher shop?"

39

ME IN THE MIRROR

A monkey saw its face in the mirror. He said to the bear, "Look at that hideous creature! How it grins and twists and turns! How ashamed I would be if I looked like that! I must confess, though, that I have seen faces just as ugly among a number of my friends!" "Don't trouble to abuse your friends," said the bear sharply; "Take a look at yourself!"

I don't know where I read this tale. In the meantime I have discovered that mirrors were already well known in the Bible. Exodus 38:8 says that the copper lavers and stands for the Tabernacle were made from the mirrors of the women who gathered at the entrance of the sanctuary. The verse shows that there were women who were concerned with their appearance. We also see that good looks were not their only concern. Their piety made them want to enhance the Tabernacle with their means.

Job 37:18 speaks of the sky being strong like a molten mirror, confirming that mirrors were made of shiny metal. Polished stone certainly had the same properties. An alternative and probably earlier mirror was clear water in which a person could see their reflection: Proverbs 27:19 speaks of "face answering face in the waters". Coating glass with gold, silver or lead became customary 2000 years ago as a product of the glass industry.

People would talk to their image in the mirror, or to the mirror itself. Often – like the monkey in the story – they were shocked at what they saw. These days we know how to distort mirror images but the fundamental basis of what we look like is still more or less recognisable.

I often meet people who say, "You're Rabbi Apple? You officiated at my Barmitzvah". Because the Barmitzvah could have been over half a century ago, I say to myself, "How old they have become!" Then I wonder what they tell themselves about how old I must now be. I see photographs of myself when I started in the ministry at the Bayswater Synagogue. What a baby face I had; and the Barmitzvah boys of those days were even more baby-faced than I. Now I am getting old (Psalm 37:25), I can't pretend any more. No longer can I say, as I guess I did at Bayswater, "I am the youngest person in Shule!" On the contrary: sometimes, as I once said at Or Hadash in Sydney, it's "I'm the oldest person here!"

I don't look too bad these days, or so I imagine. But the important thing is whether I have an old man's mentality, telling interminable stories of decades ago, always imagining that the good old days really were good. The important thing is whether, like a young man, I am still curious about the future. And whether I still want to plant metaphorical saplings even if I won't be there to see them mature.

40

AMBITIONS

Soon after landing in Sydney I revealed my plans to large gatherings of members of the Great Synagogue. A while later one of the congregation, Gerry Jurke, who knew me from Hampstead, asked, "What's happened to all your grand plans?" Answer: "They're on the way. Things take time".

I had learned (though I should have known) that imperious blasts never achieve instantaneous results. Success requires patience and perseverance, and the capacity to wait for a better time if need be. These principles I learnt from the life of Moshe Rabbenu, not that I compared myself with him.

For long periods I was the congregational *ba'al keri'ah* – the official Torah reader – which trained me in the chanting of the Torah text and constantly reminded me of Moshe Rabbenu. When I came to his final moments, I saw that however far your journey takes you, you might be denied the entry into the Promised Land. Others will – hopefully, and with God's help – have to build on your foundations and complete your work.

Should you feel cheated because the prize slips through your fingers? Should you become disillusioned and you say, "If I can't reach the goal, why did I bother in the first place?" If that's the temptation, think of the days when civilisation was on the verge of getting the first man on the moon. It took so long to make this a possibility, and there were so many false starts and failures that we might have concluded that the game, as they say, wasn't worth the candle. But at that point I heard it said that a person who tries and fails will get further than the one who says it isn't even worth trying.

The rabbinic sages said somewhat sadly, *Ein adam yotzei min ha'olam vaḥatzi ta'avato beyado*, "No-one leaves this world with even half his desires fulfilled" (Kohelet Rabbah 1:13). Everyone yearns to hand over the torch to the next generation and say, "Here you are – finish the job!" But that's not the way of wisdom. What happened at the end of Jacob's life? He summoned his family and was about to reveal his vision of what the future would hold, but, say the sages, the gift of prophecy forsook him and though he shrewdly summed up the character and capacity of each of his children he had to imply, "Now it's up to you to construct a dream and a way of your own even if it differs from mine".

We can lay good foundations but what happens when we are gone is not up to us. Ruling from the grave never really works. New ages, new stages, new pages. Others will have to pick up the torch. They probably won't handle it in the way you or I tried to. But as I used to say in the weeks before my retirement, "When I go, I have gone". The future is for others.

41

THE BISCUIT, THE HUT AND THE TRUMPET

I get mixed up when people are so selective. They put on a *tallit* but object to *tephillin*. They eat *matzah* but aren't fussy about meat. They like symbols but argue about rituals. Don't they realise that the tangible observances of Judaism give it colour, richness and personality? Florists advertise, "Say it with flowers". Our policy is, "Say it with symbols".

Judaism has a genius with symbols. It turns a dry biscuit into a *matzah*, a hut into a *sukkah*, a trumpet into a *shofar*. When I was on the staff of the Association for Jewish Youth in London, I proved my point by getting club members to write dictionary definitions. I said, "Explain *matzah*". They knew the phrase "unleavened bread", but were unsure what "unleavened" meant. They knew that *matzah* wasn't bread, at least in the regular sense. So they tried again: "*Matzah* is a dry biscuit which..." – and they got stuck. They could describe the taste, the ingredients, the shape – but the definition, and the *matzah*, had neither warmth nor personality.

We attempted the same exercise with a *sukkah*. The definitions all began, "A *sukkah* is a hut which..." Then came the same impasse. A *sukkah* is a hut - but not just a hut. The word *sukkah*, and the edifice which we call a *sukkah*, has a symbolism, a personality. A *sukkah* is more than a hut.

We tried to define a *shofar*. "A trumpet which..."? It made it easier to insert the words, "ram's horn", but once more there was no warmth, no personality. No piercing, primitive call which echoes the inner processes of the repentant human heart. No drama, no symbolism, no reminder of the historic moments where only the *shofar* could capture the moment.

The *shofar* was heard when Abraham and Isaac stood at Moriah, when God revealed Himself on Mount Sinai, when Joshua circled the walls of Jericho. Blowing the *shofar* was banned by the Romans and prohibited by the British at the Kotel; its renewal by Rav Goren in 1967 presaged the *shofar* blasts which will mark the messianic ascent of Mount Zion.

Without symbolism there is no Judaism. Rabbi Abba Hillel Silver found that his ultra-Reform congregation had banished the Torah scroll to a cellar storeroom. By rescuing the scroll, he prevented the synagogue from becoming a mere museum. It still wasn't a citadel of orthodoxy, but it regained its place in Jewish history.

If I had asked my AJY club members to define a Sefer Torah, they would have said it was "a scroll which..." They would have added words like "parchment" and "handwritten in Hebrew", but they would have recognised that what makes it a Sefer Torah is the words, the contents, the ideas – and the awesomeness, the history and feeling.

42

WHAT SORT OF JEWISH STATE?

The Arabs and the world know we are Jewish and democratic, and one day they will admit it. But "in club" let's examine what is meant by Israel's Jewishness. Historically this was always our homeland, most of its inhabitants are Jewish, its language is Hebrew, its national ways and days are Jewish. But is there a deeper reason for calling Israel "Jewish"? If you ask me why my family and I live here, it's because Israel has a Jewish mystique that enables a Jew to find him/herself. This is what I see:

- **Belief:** Ideological atheism is receding. Even those who have no room for God in their lives are searching for meaning.
- **Torah:** Whether or not they vote for religious parties or fear _haredi_ control, most Israelis have a healthy regard for tradition.
- **Jewish learning:** Torah learning is a growth industry; *yeshivot* everywhere, with a range of outlooks and ideologies - even secular ones, a sign that many are thirsty for their heritage.
- **Ethical conduct:** Chaim Weizmann wanted Israel to be "a high civilisation based on the austere standards of Jewish ethics". It is on the way, thanks to popular clamour against corruption and intolerance.
- **Spiritual/cultural creativity:** Israeli science and culture are world beaters. Even Jewish philosophy and ethics in Israel are dynamic.

- **Influence on Jews:** Israel's main *export* is not oranges but ideas and teachers. Our chief *import* is *olim*. When they criticise; let us listen.
- **Outreach to the world:** We are an inspiration to millions of gentiles, especially the Bible-lovers. Our work helps countless other nations.
- **Continuity with Jewish history:** In Israel the past lives again. Hillel and Shammai, Akiva and Rambam are more than just street names.
- **Biblical prophecy:** So much of what was foretold has come true in the way the prophets described.
- **Messianism:** For all its drawbacks, Israel has a messianic dimension. Shubert Spero said, "Jewish messianism is not identical with mere national restoration of Zion or a political ingathering, but it must certainly include these events, and the process may very well start with these events."

The sages say that redemption will come like the dawn, little by little. Israel is a Jewish State... *in the making*: a Jewish State... *on the way to fulfilling the dream.*

43

ANGLO-JEWISH COLLOQUIALISMS

I was brought up in a family that used greetings and colloquialisms brought out by their ancestors from Britain. Armed with this upbringing – with its characteristic phrases like "I wish you much joy", "Well over the fast", "Good Shobbos/Good Yuntif" – I more or less understood what was going on when I moved to London and involved myself in Anglo-Jewish life.

Even so I discovered some London Jewish idioms which puzzled me. People would speak of "The Grounds", which I eventually realised meant the cemetery. This phrase became an important to my vocabulary when I entered the ministry and spent much time at funerals and tombstone consecrations. The classy Grounds were Willesden, where the Sirs and Ladies tended to have their reserved plots. I knew I had arrived when *The Times* or *Daily Telegraph* reported an aristocratic Jewish funeral at Willesden and named me as the officiant.

Another phrase I encountered, rather less frequently, was "In *Heder*". This phrase had nothing to do with where one gained his Hebrew education. I gave a *hesped* at the *shivah* house after a certain congregant died. I will not give the person's name for reasons you will understand. I didn't know the congregant very well, though I had seen him in hospital and found him dictating business letters to his secretary whilst lying in bed (the congregant, not the secretary). Mrs. Congregant was a great worker for the Shule, and I felt I owed it to her to speak about her husband. After the service another congregant (who shall also remain anonymous in this account) said to me, "I'm surprised you spoke so nicely about him." "Why?" I asked. "Didn't you know?" came the response; "He was three times in *Heder*!" Eventually it dawned on me that *Heder* was prison. I told this to an American colleague years later, and he said that where he was brought up the term was *"Mah Nishtanah"*. He said that as a chaplain his presence was once required at a function on a Saturday. Being Shabbat he would not shave, and he was afraid that they would put him in *Mah Nishtanah*!

Popular idioms generally had to do with death, especially the greeting, "I wish you long life". Biblical thinking often used long life as a reward for piety, respect for parents, kindness to animals. It is the only reward spelt out in the Ten Commandments, though - perhaps strangely - a life cut short is not considered a punishment. When a young person dies (God forbid!) a common explanation is that the person crammed a lifetime of good deeds into a short time, or that God took them before they were tempted to commit transgressions. There is a wonderful saying, "Only God can put years into your life: only you can put life into your years".

44

PAYING YOUR TAXES

The historic Jewish community of Goulburn in southern New South Wales has long disbanded, though a few Jewish individuals and families live in the district. Some belong to the Southern Highlands community, which I used to visit about once a year and for whom I consecrated a cemetery. There is a Goulburn property – once owned by Jews - with an old edifice in its grounds that might have been a private synagogue, though the community as such probably never built a house of worship. Thinking of Goulburn recalls a well known 19th century saying which comes at the end of this particular chapter, so bear with me whilst I get there.

Let me first remark that being part of society comes at a cost. There is a famous *halakhic* rule stated in the name of the 3rd century sage Sh'muel, *dina d'malkhuta dina*, "The law of the land is the law". It comes four times in the Talmud and is endorsed in every code of Jewish law.

There can be – and is - discussion about the parameters of this rule, but it certainly includes a duty to pay taxes. There can be – and is - debate as to how much tax should be levied on a person, but the principle of taxation is beyond *halakhic* question and the non-payment of taxes is a form of stealing (*Shulḥan Arukh, Ḥoshen Mishpat* 369:6). Failure to meet one's tax obligations is morally and legally wrong, a *Ḥillul HaShem*, a desecration of God's Name (Maimonides, *Hilkhot Gezelah* 5:11, *Kesef Mishnah*).

This includes "fiddling the books" and falsifying a tax return. Both are a grave infraction of the law against stealing, a desecration of God's Name. A Jew must be scrupulously honest in every aspect of life. Ordinary citizens, the "little people", complain that whilst they try to be honest, they see "the big boys" successfully rorting the system. Judaism is adamant that "the big boys" will not escape Divine punishment even if for a time they succeed in evading the law of the land. There is no reason to refuse any validly allowed deduction, but concealing or distorting the facts cannot be *halakhically* justified. For example, if you claim a deduction for a charitable donation, you have to be able to prove that you really did give to the charity.

So now we come to the 19th century saying. In those days Australia had a byword, "As honest as a Goulburn Jew". Everyone should remember this saying and conduct themselves so uprightly that people will say, "As honest as a Jew". This is the exact opposite of the anti-Semitic canard, "Jews love money, Jews will defraud you, Jews can't be trusted." The antisemites always twist the truth (that's the irrational nature of their affliction). Let our own actions prove the antisemites wrong.

45

BAR-CELONA

My subject is not the drinking-holes of Barcelona or anywhere else. My concern is more serious and arose out of the few days we spent in Spain not long ago prior to a Mediterranean cruise. The ship left from Barcelona on a Sunday; we arrived the previous Wednesday and spent Shabbat at a hotel near the local Chabad house. Over 100 people attended the Friday night and Shabbat morning services – locals as well as tourists – and we learned that the city has at least two other synagogues, as well as kosher restaurants and shops. There are also Jewish communities in Madrid and elsewhere.

There is a popular view that after the expulsion from Spain in 1492, the Jewish people enacted a *herem* against Spain, barring Jews (that's where I get the term "bars" in my title) from entering the country henceforth. The popular view has no basis. In an article in 1967, C.C. Aronsfeld recorded that he had examined a string of works on Spanish Jewish history, and none confirmed the existence of a *herem*. Naturally, Jews were loath to return to the scene of such aggression against a solid community that had brought so much benefit to Spain, but there does not seem to have been a formal *herem*.

The "*herem*" was probably merely a warning to Jews to keep away from the dangers of the Inquisition. The decree of expulsion sent large numbers of Jews in other directions. The lands to which they brought their talents and energies included Holland and England, forming also the basis of the Jewish community of the United States. By the early 18th century Jews were back in Spain, largely drawn by material factors. By the 19th century there was a growing spirit of tolerance. As the Inquisition waned, Jews were allowed to hold their own opinions and practise their own rites. Today Chabadniks walk the streets of Barcelona, and Jews come from all over the world for the football – or at least to embark on a Mediterranean cruise.

When we were in Gibraltar on our honeymoon, we crossed into Spain and stayed in Torremolinos. We still remember the quality and cheapness of Spanish tailoring, and the excited women with live chickens on the Spanish buses. We still don't know much Spanish, though we learned enough to order two cups of tea with milk and to more or less follow the Chabad rabbi's sermon in Barcelona. It helps to have a general idea of some of the European languages, though Hungarian baffled us not only in Budapest but in Sydney in the days of the Hungarian Jewish immigration. I would never have handled the Hungarian documents brought to me by prospective brides and grooms if not for my colleague Rev. Isidor Gluck, who knew so many languages that when he was visiting Jewish patients in hospitals the nurses enlisted his talents in interpreting for the non-Jews too.

46

JUDAISM WITHOUT GOD

Soon after my debate about God with an Australian humanist, my opponent attended a service at my synagogue. I asked him, "Did you like the sermon?"; he said, "Thank God!" In the USA, Sherwin Wine, the rabbi of the atheists, did not claim to be an atheist himself but said he was just not sure. I wonder what he felt about life after death. I guess we can't look for him in *Olam HaBa* to find if his view has changed.

How many people are not sure about God? Forget statistics. One's thinking never stands still, and people are often ready to give God the benefit of the doubt by the time they die. Rav Kook said that if anyone agonises over whether they believe in God, it shows that they have a glimmer of a thought that maybe the Almighty does exist after all.

Some Jews deny God because they are angry. Yet if there is no God, who is there to be angry with? Jews have often confronted God, and said, "If God lived in my village, I would break all His windows". When a navy chaplain asked me, "It's hard to fathom how God runs the world, but we keep our doubts to ourselves. What do you Jews say? May one shout at God?" I told him that Judaism does so constantly; the Talmud says, "*Zo Torah v'zu secharah* - Is this religion, and is this its reward?" In some texts God replies, "Silence! This is My decree!" (In the liturgy, He says, "Silence, or I will turn the world back to water!"). When Job tries to sue God, he gets a tongue-lashing. In our generation He is more likely to say with the Bible, "*Yadati b'ni yadati* – I know, My child, I know…" We have problems, but He won't let us remain bereft, lost in a cold, unfeeling world.

It is said Wine deleted God from his *siddur*, removed the Ark from his synagogue, and made man the measure of all things. How did Wine cope if God was no longer the central character in Jewish history? What did he do with the feeling of realms above and beyond the earthbound and human? How did he handle life's mystery, mystique and transcendence? If he abdicated and said, "I state no view", how could he call himself a leader, a guide? If he said, "I leave it to you to find your own answers", isn't this tantamount to making himself redundant? Rabbis dare not opt out.

Any individual can try to live without God, but Judaism as a whole can't. Elie Wiesel said, "A Jew can be *for* God, a Jew can be *against* God, a Jew cannot be *without* God". According to the rabbis, God says, "Let them forget Me, but keep My commandments". This implies, "You can live as a Jew without mentioning Me". But if you live as a Jew, how can you *not* mention God?

47

GOD SITS BESIDE ME

In synagogues with set seating, people are curious as to who has been allocated the vacant seat next to them. Members of a family get het up about an outsider entering a family preserve. It's not just that we regard our row in the synagogue as our own private turf, but if an outsider gets in we wonder how we will ever be able to talk to them.

You shouldn't be talking to your Shule neighbours anyhow, but life being what it is, very few people resist the temptation to have a chat during the service, at least the more boring parts. Actually there's nothing wrong with chatting in Shule, so long as the chat is to yourself – part of the introspection of the High Holyday season – or better still, to God. In fact, I used to tell people, try to imagine that it's God who is sitting beside you.

From the theological point of view, that's almost heresy. How can one use the term "sitting" in regard to a God who has no bodily form or shape, who is incapable of earthly actions like sitting or standing, or of human feelings like joy, anger, hope or disappointment? Philosophers such as Abraham Joshua Heschel explain these phenomena in detail.

Whilst Maimonides denies that God has personal characteristics, Samson Raphael Hirsch in the 19th century believes this goes too far. According to Hirsch, removing personality from God is untrue to history and a threat to Judaism. Though God is certainly not a person, we can relate to Him only if we speak to Him as a person. Otherwise how can we say *Barukh Attah,* "Blessed art Thou?" How can we address Him at all or think of Him as a Presence? How can we regard Him as being interested in us as individuals?

This is not to say that God is corporeal. Yes, there were thinkers, especially in medieval France, who were corporealists. Moses of Taku said God could assume human form if He desired. Isaiah of Trani thought He was made of an ethereal substance without human frailties or limitations. Some even felt that Rashi was a corporealist: an interesting question, but anyone who promotes Divine corporeality these days would be a heretic.

Fundamentally, applying human terms to God (anthropomorphism, anthropopathism) is merely poetry, part of the world of metaphor, not to be taken literally. When we say that God is *with us*, when we talk of *the hand of God* or *the mouth of God*, we don't mean it in a literal sense. Phrases like these are useful because they are helpful. God is too vast and infinite to be captured on the small screen, but when Harold Kushner (in "Why Bad Things Happen to Good People") speaks of Him sitting *shivah* beside us we begin to sense His reality.

48

BABIES TO ORDER

How to choose a baby's gender is an old subject. Studying Talmudic material about conception and pregnancy (e.g. Yevamot 12a/b), the sages of various generations put forward advice on how to ensure without medical intervention that a child will be of a particular gender. At Dayan Kaplin's *shi'urim* at Etz Hayyim Yeshivah in Golders Green, I raised various questions, and the next day Rabbi Kaplin brought me a booklet that claimed medical validity for the sages' theories, but I decided not to ask our family doctor to comment.

Years later I found an analysis in J. David Bleich's *Judaism and Healing: Halakhic Perspectives*, 1981, p. 111. The main principle is that cohabitation should occur naturally. Every child brings its own blessing into the world. Whatever sex a baby is, it must be welcomed and loved ("Genetic Screening and Pre-Implantation Sex Selection in *Halakhah*" by Richard V. Grazi and Joel B. Wolowelsky in *Le'ela* 36, 1993).

Halakhah does not automatically rule out today's sophisticated scientific techniques, but subjects them to moral considerations. Rabbi Immanuel Jakobovits warned against "babies on demand", in the sense of creating a particular number and type of babies – for instance, tall, strong, blond children to populate the nation and its army, to strengthen a political party. or to eliminate "undesirables", e.g. females, homosexuals, gypsies, coloureds or Jews, or people with mental or medical handicaps. Yet though he was wary of "wish lists", Lord Jakobovits said, "There is no moral objection in principle to genetic engineering or manipulation" ("In Vitro Fertilisation and Genetic Engineering", a 1984 report).

He added: "The critical difference is between 'improving' nature and correcting it (or between positive and negative eugenics). The elimination of any abnormality or defect to ensure the health of children to be born is morally no different from any other medical or surgical intervention to overcome nature's disabilities. Such acts of healing, whether performed on organs, limbs or genes, are included in the Biblical sanction or dispensation granted to doctors. But this licence does not cover acts of intervention of nature lacking therapeutic justification."

There could be therapeutic justification for helping couples who have fertility problems or wish to prevent genetic diseases. This is better than waiting until a woman is already pregnant and then talking about abortion. If the motivation is social, including creating embryos in order to harvest their parts, Judaism is wary: children should be valued for themselves, not as a bag of spare parts.

49

FORGIVENESS

On Kol Nidre night I generally began my sermon by asking the congregation to forgive anything which I may have said or not said to them, done or not done. There is a saying attributed to Alexander Pope, "To err is human: to forgive, divine". It is lovely rhetoric, but it makes assumptions which are not entirely warranted. "To err is human" echoes the Christian doctrine of Original Sin, which says that because we descend from Adam who sinned, we are all born tainted, and to err is our nature. On thether hand, Judaism knows that we sin, but it's not because we have to. We sometimes miss the mark, not because it is a necessary part of being human. Nazis were cruel not because they were humans but because they found it easier to heed Big Brother and ignore their conscience. If pressed they might blame the system, but did they know the rule of Elazar ben Durdaya in the Talmud (A.Z. 17a) who recognised that he had to stop blaming others and accept that "everything depends on me myself"? No-one has to go along with wrongdoing. He should have the moral courage to resist, whatever the cost.

What do we say about "To forgive (is) divine"? Certainly forgiveness is a basic quality of the Almighty. But is His forgiveness an act of grace, or must the sinner show a sign of remorse, a beginning, however small, to which God can respond: "Return to Me, and I shall return to you" (Mal. 3:7)? Jewish thinking prefers the second view. Were the Nazis at all ashamed of their actions, and anxious for atonement? If they remained unrepentant, even proud of their deeds, how could God forgive them?

97

Whom did they offend more – God, or other humans? It hardly matters. An offence against any of God's creatures wounds God too. We need not ask whether a Nazi was officially a religious believer (presumably a Christian) giving lip service to Biblical teaching: surely his faith had ethical principles. Defaming the person also defames God. Can and should the victim of a Nazi's cruelty forgive him? The ethic that calls God forgiving expects us to be forgiving too: "As He is merciful, so should you be merciful". No-one should obstinately withhold forgiveness, be obsessed with revenge or retaliation, or rejoice when an enemy falls. But turning the other cheek goes too far. "Forgiving" one Nazi might make it easier between you and him, but it's not just you and him. What about the other Nazis, the other victims, the world as a whole?

All this takes us beyond the issue of forgiveness between rabbi and congregation. But even the smallest sin can cause a moral tsunami. Rebbe Nahman of Breslov used to say, "If it is possible to cause damage, it is possible to repair damage".

50

HANUKAH AND CHRISTMAS

Some Christians (as well as the media) think that Hanukah is the Jewish Christmas. Some Jews think that Christmas is the Christian Hanukah. Both are wrong. The two festivals are unrelated even though they sometimes occur at the same time. Christmas is a *Christian* occasion though it gets the date wrong, since 25 December has no connection to Jesus' real date of birth and he was actually born in 3 or 4 BCE. Hanukah, with all its universalistic message of freedom of conscience, is a *Jewish* event. It has its own narrative, its own cast of characters, its own mode of celebration.

There is an immense amount of Christmas hype in the December air, and there are some Jews who get caught up in the celebrations. But Santa Claus, Christmas carols and holly leaves are out of place for Jews. Judaism does not pay homage to Christ. His birthday – whenever the date might be - is irrelevant for Jews. Mutual respect does not require glossing over differences. Nor does it help to say that Christmas is now a secular event dedicated to the shops. What an insult to Christianity! No wonder that at times in my career I stood up and stood out in protest against such things.

When Rev. Fred Nile started an organisation in Australia called Festival of Light, he hijacked a name that belonged to almost every people and faith: all in some way have a contrast of darkness and light. The Dead Sea Scrolls, for example, feature the conflict of Sons of Light and Sons of Darkness. Light opens the Bible and permeates Jewish practice. The Eternal Light symbolised God's presence in the sanctuary; the Temple invaders tried to quench Judaism by extinguishing the light, and the Maccabees made the rekindling of the *ner tamid* a priority. When Fred Nile ran a conference about Soviet Jewry I was one of the speakers, but other times I felt I had no choice but to oppose what he was doing, such as a street parade in which so-called Messianic Jews walked ahead of the marchers blowing *shofarot*.

There is a view that H̲anukah echoes a pagan sun festival. This can'tbe correct since it is independent of the solar months. Solar calendars are an eccentric feature of ancient Jewish history with little enduring significance.

Christianity had a doctrine of Jesus as "Light of the World"; some of the saints saw Jesus as the new sun. Associating his birth with midwinter invited the symbolism of a flash of light. It also echoed the Roman idea of the unconquered sun. There is no law against two feasts of light at the same season, but coincidence does not make them interchangeable. Still, what preserved H̲anukah and made it so popular may be its proximity to Christmas. Maybe it was a cultural compensation for Jews.

51

COMPUTERS

I came late to computers. Riva studied the subject at university and all my children and grandchildren mastered the art, but it was a mystery to me until the 1990s when Professor Alan Crown talked me into buying a laptop. I still don't know how computers work, but I can do word processing. Marian, who taught me email and the Internet, now says, "He's on it all day!"

The laptop I use is probably our fourth. I am so attached to it that its imminent retirement will be a wrench. Like my car. I didn't have a car until 1967 – actually the first day of the Six-Day War. The car's first outing was when my father and I drove to the Albert Hall for the communal rally. Over the years I loved my car of the moment, and before our Aliyah I sold our lovely secondhand Lexus. We offered it to Bensi, but he had nowhere to park it. In Israel we don't have a car. In England a few years ago we hired one but driving into and out of London was too hard for my nerves.

Thanks to Bensi I can use a computer to write our weekly *OzTorah*, now well into its third decade with hundreds of email subscribers all over the world. I am the writer and Bensi is the editor/publisher. People urged me to turn the *OzTorahs* into a book and I did this, producing *Let's Ask the Rabbi*, though I have no idea how many of our subscribers made the effort to buy it from the online booksellers. On the other hand there are periodicals in Israel, Australia and elsewhere which syndicate my material. People sometimes say, "I enjoyed your article this week!" and I used to reply, "What did I write?" because the publishers use the archive without always telling me in advance. However, when I said, "What did I write?" it was thought that I was being modest, so I now simply say, "Thankyou!"

Writing comes easily to me. I once dreamt of being a famous author but I no longer believe in fame, and of course my type of subject will never be a best-seller. I do a lot of research and even get into the academic journals, but books are harder because publishers want subsidies. Lodge Mark Owen in Sydney sponsored one of my Masonic books and the Museum of Freemasonry another, but other manuscripts sit there awaiting sponsors.

Like everyone else I find that my computer tends to have a mind of its own. Almost always my granddaughter Shaina can fix the problem in the proverbial jiffy. None of my grandchildren is frightened by the computer, but I still am. In an earlier book I wrote about Davoru's early computer which was so big and heavy that when he left its constituent parts in our attic in Potts Point, it nearly broke my back to lug the stuff down the stairs to the garbage when the time came to throw it out. If we had waited, Davoru could have sold it as a historical relic.

52

SHOULD WE SEEK CONVERTS?

Our numbers, lower than pre-Holocaust, are not growing. It would help if Jewish couples had more children, but that is unlikely outside the strictly orthodox. It would be good if more Jews came back to their identity, but, already Jewish, they will not increase our numbers though they will strengthen our quality. What about conversionist outreach? The Bible knows two types of converts - the *ger toshav*, the "resident alien" living "Jewish-style", and the *ger tzedek*, the full convert, who echoes Ruth: "Where you go I will go; where you dwell I will dwell; your people will be my people, your God will be my God" (Ruth 1:16-17). Maimonides wrote (*Issurei Bi'ah* 13:1-4), that a convert re-enacts Sinai through circumcision if a male; immersion ("sanctify yourself"); bringing a sacrifice; and accepting the Torah ("we shall do, we shall listen").

In Roman times the 8 million Jews included many converts; others were "God-fearers" (Num. R. 8:2; *Mekhilta Mishpatim* 18; *Avot d'Rabbi Natan*, A:36/B:18, Acts 13:16, 26) who "accepted Judaism as a great and beautiful ideal but did not become complete Jews" (J. Klausner). The Gospels are scathing: "Woe to you, scribes and Pharisees, hypocrites! You compass sea and land to make one proselyte" (Matt. 13:15). Salo Baron thinks Judaism was attractive because it offered stability, spirituality, rationality and morality. Josephus reports, like Greek and Latin authors, that "the masses show a keen desire to adopt our religious observances". Despite *dicta* such as "one welcomes a proselyte so as to bring him under the wings of the Divine Presence" (Lev.R. 2:9), some converts lapsed (*Gitt.*

45b etc.). Some compared proselytes to a *sappaḥat* or boil (*Yev.* 47b etc.) - a play on Isaiah (14:1), who said *v'nis'p'ḥu*: "They *cleave like a sore* to the House of Israel".

Judaism now said "the pious of the nations" need only the seven Noaḥide laws (Maimonides, *Melakhim* 8:10). But the sages refused "to close the door before proselytes" (*Mekhilta, Mishpatim* 18) and converts continued to arrive, like the Eastern European Khazars. But Jews (e.g. in Cromwell's England) often avoided proselytisation for fear of offending the host society. Today there is new interest, which I support, in seeing Judaism as an idea whose time has come. The world would gain from Jewish pragmatic holiness, social cohesion and messianic striving. There are practical and *halakhic* problems in a conversion campaign, though the sages said, "God exiled Israel among the nations in order to augment their numbers through proselytes" (Pes. 87b). If a gentile is not ready for full Judaism, why not increase the "friends of Judaism"? As Elie Wiesel says, our task is not to Judaise the world but to *make it more human*.

53

THE BIBLE BORROWING FROM ITSELF

The older I get, the more I like the Bible. Not only for what it says, but because it borrows from itself. An example is the Book of Esther, which describes life in Shushan in terms that are reminiscent of the Joseph stories in Genesis. Two examples are the king's dream and the obeisance given to a ruler. In the second case we see the author's skilful handling of words and events and his delicate use of humour when the tables are turned on Haman.

Dreams play a major role in the Bible. Joseph's youthful dreams cause havoc in the family. The butler and baker have life-changing dreams. Pharaoh has dreams about things that play on his mind. Since night-time dreams deal with day-time concerns, kings dream about economic issues, wheat, meat, supply and demand. If you ask today's people what they dream about, some will say they never dream, which is highly unlikely; others know they had a dream but remember nothing. It is likely that politicians dream of party and parliamentary issues, educators of classrooms and curricula, doctors of patients and potions; rabbis dream of synagogues and other rabbis. But dreams are not visions. Dreams usually happen at night: visions are day-time flights of fancy. Dreams mostly take no account of realities: visions do.

When Joseph's brothers enter his presence as Prime Minister of Egypt they bow to the ground in his honour (Gen. 42:6). Why do they enter his presence at all, since it is unlikely that everyone who came to buy corn was personally received by Joseph? Perhaps the state officials are suspicious of a large group of foreigners and want Joseph to decide. The Midrash (Gen. R. 91:4) says that the brothers have been asking around in case their long-lost brother is somewhere in Egypt. Their activities come to Joseph's ears and he guesses what is going on, so he arranges to see them and determine whether they have repented.

Both aspects of the Joseph saga suggest a shape for the Purim story. Earlier narratives, as well as poetry and prose from other parts of the Bible, constantly find their echo in the later Books. The Books of Kings and Chronicles handle the same events and interpret them from their own angle.

One of the subjects I am currently researching is the Psalms as Midrash. I have found so many events in the early part of Tanakh reflected and reflected upon in the Book of Tehillim. In most cases the Psalmist puts a slant on the earlier material and sometimes opens the door for *midrashic* analysis. There are conclusions that this material suggests, in both style and substance. I am not yet ready to draw the conclusions, but I dream of the time at which I will be able to do so.

54

THE JEWS AND THE JESUITS

Much of my life has focussed on interfaith, intercommunity understanding and co-operation. I have constantly seen how different one Christian group is from another. An important instance is the Jesuits – Catholics but a distinctive sub-group of the Catholic Church. What a paradox: on the one hand, a Christian claim that the Jesuit movement is too pro-Jewish; on the other, a Jewish allegation that it is antisemitic.

Their official name is Society of Jesus. Critics called them "Jesuits" in a derogatory sense, arguing that the Society misappropriated the name of Jesus. Created in Paris in 1534 by Ignatius of Loyola, one of its aims was hospital and missionary work in Jerusalem, though later it concentrated on Europe. In 1543 Ignatius established in Rome a home for converted Jews, and the Jesuits debated whether former Jews could become members.

The 16th century was difficult for both Christians and Jews. Luther challenged conventional Christianity; the Inquisition and the expulsion of Spanish Jewry left many Jews feeling fragile. A German general, Erich Ludendorff, claimed that the Society of Jesus had been created by Jews with papal support in order to undermine Luther and rule the world.

The Nazis added the Freemasons to their black list of those making common cause with the Jews and the Jesuits, leading to complaints that Freemasons were too *pro*-Jewish - or too *anti*-Jewish. There was a Jewish connection with Jesuit beginnings. The family of Diego (Jaime) Laynez, Loyola's successor, was probably originally Jewish, like Juan Alonso de Polanco, Loyola's secretary. Loyola himself regretted that he was not "a blood relative of the Lord". He allowed "new Christians" into the order; in 1552 he admitted Giovanni Baptista Eliano, a grandson of the Hebraist scholar, Elijah Levita. By late 16th century, however, the order turned against "new Christians" and by 1608 its rules required at least five generations of Christian identity. This restriction was not removed until 1946.

The claim that the order was anti-Jewish cites Jesuit antagonism to Jews in 18th century Poland, even though the Society had earlier attacked the Portuguese Inquisition. There was Jesuit opposition to Alfred Dreyfus in late 19th century France, despite there being pro-Dreyfus Jesuits too.

More significant is the antisemitism of some Jesuit publications prior to 1946, though the Society opposed the Nazi racist doctrines and a leading Jesuit, Cardinal Bea, was a proponent of rapprochement with the Jews.

Both Jesuits and Jews have been accused of seeking world domination. Both indignantly insist that their motives are beyond question and they are only interested in teaching spiritual and ethical ideals.

55

DEATH WITH DIGNITY

Knowing that the sages said, "Wise people, be careful with your words" (Avot 1:11), I have an obsession with choosing the right word – and an aversion to words being distorted. I can't fathom how people can say that a child born out of wedlock is a "love child" or that euthanasia is "dying with dignity"... A character in "Alice in Wonderland" says that words mean what he chooses them to mean. When he says "black", he really means "white". When he says "hard" he means "soft". The Talmud had no patience for such ideas. It said, "Let your *yea* be a *yea* and your *nay* be a *nay*". But the real danger is not from extremes of this kind but arises when a word bears a nuance which is not in itself illogical but is tendentious, like describing stealing as "liberating". It is a breach of the Ninth Commandment – "Do not bear false witness".

If I take the "love child" example, I make no judgment about whether a couple who have a baby when they are not married to each other are bound by love. But since when is the child of a *married* couple not "a love child"? What has happened to the idea that a couple choose each other out of love, marry and live together out of love, share marital intimacy out of love, and express their love in a family which will broaden their love and enhance the world? The "love child" phrase was invented by the media, always looking for quick catchwords. I'm not sure if it was the media who dubbed Israel "an apartheid state", but if it was, it is a criminal distortion of a word that means something quite different and arose in quite different circumstances. Why do this to Israel, which for all its faults is far from apartheid? It's like the movie mogul (that phrase too is a media invention) who said when he made a film about Moses, "Moses, I made you – and I can break you!" The misuse of words has given us freedom which is closer to slavery, peace which is closer to war, riches which are closer to poverty...

At the other end of life's scale, "dying with dignity" is said by some to be what happens when a person goes in for "assisted suicide". Does this mean that someone who dies a "normal" death when life ebbs and they drift away has not died "with dignity"? A French writer says that what we fear is not death but dying. Whether *death* has a dignity we won't discover until the next world. We ought to be praying that our *dying* will be with dignity.

The twisting of speech makes words dangerous. No wonder the Bible says that "death and life are in the power of the tongue" (Prov. 18:21). No wonder the great theme of the Talmud is words: constantly weighing up the words of Scripture and the commentary that followed it. Moses said he was not "a man of words" (Ex. 4:10) but that's not always a thing to boast about.

56

WHERE SHOULD THE CLERGY BE?

Don't think that in ancient Israel the priests were confined to a fixed location in the sanctuary. They had a wider role. They supervised public health and provided counselling. However, they worked within set parameters, and it was the prophets who spoke out and goaded the government. Some prophets were priests, but generally there was a division of labour. By Roman times prophecy had more or less waned, and the priests stepped out of their conventional confines to become the formal face of the community, though some were mercenaries who toadied to the regime.

In modern democracies the clergy go everywhere and speak out on everything. Not without controversy. When they involve themselves in national debate, there are vested interests that feel threatened. Voices are raised: "Back to your Bible! Stick to your sermons! Keep to your altar!"

In my case I had a view on everything and wasn't afraid to articulate it. In Britain, my views on racism got quoted in the House of Lords. I was summoned to the Race Relations Board because of views expressed as chairman of the Jewish Marriage Council. In Australia I weighed into countless public debates - on radio and TV, in the print media and on an array of public platforms. Should Australians keep the Queen? Should abortion be available? Should the unemployed do voluntary work for the dole? Should the media peddle smut? Should sports teams pray for a win? Should politicians take courses in civics (and civility)? Should gays parade in the streets? Should advertisers tell the truth? Should immigration be controlled? Should rich nations help poor ones? Issues like these.

Generally there were no grumbles from the Jewish community: I was careful not to let the side down, though when I took up a position on Aboriginal welfare, one of my congregation refused to come to Shule unless I kept quiet. I occasionally received threats to my life but apart from taking obvious precautions I just kept going with my normal activities. Naturally some whose toes I trod on said clergy should stick to teaching the Bible. My answer was that this actually *was* "teaching the Bible". This is what the Bible is about – justice, peace and truth. The Biblical prophets constantly risked persecution because they would not hold their tongues.

When film stars and swimmers made statements on education and the economy I objected that they had no special qualifications in these areas – but in regard to the quality of society, this is precisely where the clergy *do* have special qualifications. Bringing what they see as Biblical truth into the market-place of ideas is not just being nosy. Archbishop Temple used to say that God is interested in a lot of other things besides religion.

57

THE JEWISH TUNIC

British Jewry and its offshoots used to be adamant that the clergy should be properly attired in caps and gowns, often with preacher's bands and clerical collars too. Not only the clergy but the top-hatted and gowned beadles (British congregations did not use the term *shammash* or *shammas*). Honorary Officers had to wear black jackets, striped trousers (no-one usually asked about *sha'atnez*, a forbidden mixture of wool and linen) and top hats.

The first time I decked myself out as a minister I borrowed a (misshapen) minister's cap from somewhere and added the academic gown which I had acquired as a university graduate. In time I bought a minister's black cap and gown and white bands from Ede and Ravenscroft in the West End, plus a white cap and gown for the High Holydays and a clerical collar. When I got married, Marian made me some white lace bands, utilising the design used at the Spanish and Portuguese Synagogue. The bands came into synagogue life from the law and academia, though some people argued that they represented the two tablets of the Ten Commandments...

All this is part of the Anglo-Jewish interpretation of the saying, "manners maketh man". The ministerial garb also expressed another saying, "clothes make the man", but this suggests that only when you are dressed do you look like a real person. Ex. 39:22 uses the phrase *me'il ha-ephod*, "robe of the ephod". This was a long flowing robe worn by men of high status, a formal garment made of pure blue, with the hem decorated with alternating bells and blue "pomegranates". Blue was always regarded as a rich, important colour. The new profession called colour psychology sees blue as man's favourite colour. In Judaism it was said that blue represents the sea and the sky, symbolic of the idea that God rules below and above.

Beneath the robe was probably some kind of tunic. Men engaged in menial work needed a practical garment like an apron, with at least one pocket to house their work tools. An under-garment could have been worn under the tunic. Garments of all kinds were a mark of identity and rank.

In later times there were rabbinical robes which indicated one's dignity. The sages even said that a *talmid ḥakham* with a spot on his clothes deserved to die. These days, rabbinical robes for synagogue wear have largely disappeared but the casual clothing that some modern rabbis adopt can go too far in the direction of informality. I brought my white vestments to Israel with me but have never used them. The black ones remain, probably gathering dust, in Sydney.

58

WHAT IS GOD?

When I was a child I thought my rabbi standing in his pulpit was God. Years later I found that Tennyson said that the average Englishman's idea of God was of an immeasurable clergyman. In time I became a clergyman myself, and despite whatever self-confidence I possessed I knew I was far from Divine. At times I even worried if I was human enough.

Even before I became a rabbi I talked about (and to) God, but I never succeeded in reaching a definition. I toyed with calling Him "The Great Idea", but I realised He is more than an abstract theory or hypothesis. In Buber-like terms that is like calling Him "The Great It". I thought of describing Him as "The Great Force", but despite His creativity He is more than just a fount of energy. Calling Him "The Great Presence" says nothing of His capacity to create, to criticise, to reveal His will. Calling Him "The Cosmic Grandfather", which, to borrow Buber again, makes Him "The Great Thou", gives Him benignness but makes Him too cosy and cuddly. A Christian colleague told me he sees God as a heavenly Santa Claus. A rabbi whose English was a bit shaky thought of Psalm 23 when he told his congregation, "You will be my ship and I will be your ship-herd". Whilst not judging the sheep-shepherd duality as an approach to the rabbi-synagogue situation, calling God "The Great Shepherd" has its limitations.

We all have our own take on God. No-one can define Him with accuracy and authority. Hebrew theologians say, "If I knew Him, I would be Him".

The Hebrew benediction formula addresses Him in both the second and third person, as You and He at one and the same time, symbolising the polarity of a God who is both near and far, both immanent and transcendent.

I eventually gave up the attempt at definitions, largely because none gave me a God I could relate to or who could relate to me. Then I recalled that when Moses asked God who He was, the response was, "I am what I am".

The Bible often says "*and*" – "*And* the Lord spoke", "*And* these are the laws", "*And* Jacob dwelt". Belief in God is a relationship, a set of "*ands*": God *and* the world, God *and* humanity, God *and* our destiny. Because of God, my life is different – and makes a difference. I am not always certain which way to turn, but my belief helps me through the options. I am not always strong enough to do the right thing, but my belief enables me to rise above my own frailty and the moral weakness of others. I do not always like what I find in the world, but when I see evil, my belief gives me no rest until I cry out. I demand an explanation, but maybe it's sometimes better not to have one. I have enough faith in God to know that He is bigger and wiser than me.

59

PRETENDING TO READ MUSIC

Music was never my strong point. Though I can more or less hold a tune I have never been a singer, though in an emergency I have had to stand in for the *ḥazzan*. In Sydney I had a copy of the choir music book and on High Holydays I pretended to be following the scores, but it was all a show. Nonetheless – perhaps under the influence of the late Toddy Simons - I became a devotee of the stately but rather plain Anglo-Jewish musical tradition, which now only persists in patches. My ideal *ḥazzan* is not a florid improviser/impresario but a pleasant prayer leader who maintains the accepted shape of the service without vocal theatrics.

In synagogue life I believed in an interaction between sound and sight, song and speech; chanting texts, not just reading them. I found that that people who gave up strict observance and rarely attended synagogue, retained snatches of liturgical melody.

There is a *Midrash* that Jewish history can be seen as a song. Adam sang when Shabbat was created; the end of days will be one great psalm of thankfulness. Musical instruments were invented at the beginning of time. Moses' majestic *Shirat HaYam* will be replicated at the final redemption. Women sang as well as men: witness the Song of Deborah. The Temple had sacrifice – and song. The Levites looked after the ritual – and the music. David was the great king – and composer. When God wanted the Messiah to come from the family of King Hezekiah, the angels stood up for David: "Hezekiah," they told the Almighty, "never composed a song in his life!"

J.G. Frazer says in "The Golden Bough", "The musician has done his part as well as the prophet in the making of religion. Every faith has its appropriate music, and the difference between the creeds might almost be expressed in musical notation". More: the influence of musical modes on each other, and the integration of secular folk melody, are part of the story.

Mourning was the counter-experience to joy. When an individual or nation was bereft they had no song on their lips. By the waters of Babylon our tormentors wanted the songs of Zion we had no song in our hearts. Music in Eastern Europe had a melancholy and minor key. It hoped for release but found repression. That's why *hazzanut* moved from one emotion to another, now sweet and joyful, now bitter and lachrymose. We wept at Zion ruined; we laughed and dreamed of Zion rebuilt.

Friday nights - and many other days too - see me in my synagogue in Jerusalem. The place resounds to the sound of music. Though life is so often fraught and fragile, my heart is released by song. I may be out of tune but I sing along.

60

TRAVEL AND EXPENSE ACCOUNTS

When I read Nahum Goldmann's biography I discovered what a great Jewish leader and ambassador Goldmann was. He held so many positions that it was even said that in inter-organisation discussions each side was represented by Nahum Goldmann and Nahum Goldmann, and it was as if Goldmann was negotiating with himself. Goldmann was a well-to-do person and I think he met his own expenses. He seems to have paid for his own accommodation and travel, and took no salary. People lacking private resources were not in the same position and the organisations they served had to fund their expenses.

This was certainly the situation with me. I had two full-time jobs - senior rabbi of the Great Synagogue, and communal rabbinic spokesman and ambassador. The Shule funded my congregational duties without complaint or question, but much of my representational activity had no financial support (though the Defence Force funded my military work). When I travelled throughout Australia and New Zealand, the communities concerned facilitated my visits, but I had to find my own means to carry out speaking engagements for public bodies including churches and lodges. Rev. Gluck quoted what he had heard in Ireland, "If you want to do work for nothing you'll never be idle!" I was certainly never idle, though I did often feel tired.

The *halakhic* writing about rabbinic salaries says one should not make the Torah "a spade to dig with" (Avot 4:5). According to the sages, God says, "Just as I gave the Torah gratis, so you should convey the Torah without payment". Talmudic rabbis were hewers of wood, drawers of water, even a gladiator. A few received payment for technical work such as the scribal arts. By the Middle Ages, life was so pressured that if rabbis did not get paid there would be no rabbis. A concept developed that a rabbi should be compensated for being unable to work at another profession. In my case I said that if I were not a rabbi I could have become a top barrister and should be paid according to barristers' scales. No-one agreed...

Some communal professionals receive massive amounts. I was never so lucky. Indeed bearing in mind the pressure and hours of the job, the pay was mediocre. I recall being told patronisingly that it was a privilege to serve the community. Actually there was a hint of that when the United Synagogue honorary officers met a rabbinic delegation including me about salary scales. The US president, Sir Isaac Wolfson, asked my colleague Cyril Harris, "Rabbi Harris, how much are we paying you?" Hearing the reply, Sir Isaac was honest enough to say, "My doorman gets more than you do!"

61

WOULD I DO IT AGAIN?

When Maimonides codifies the laws of penitence, he says that the sign of true repentance is that if you had the chance again, you would not repeat the same sin. With this in mind let me answer the question that I was often asked, "Would you be a rabbi again if you had the choice?" It's not that being a rabbi is a sin, but some rabbis live to regret their choice of career and go into other things. I saw when we joined Bet Yosef Synagogue in Israel that they had a number of ex-rabbis, but I was the only one who lasted the distance in the pulpit. Others went into law, education, fundraising, administration, and other professions. Did I remain a rabbi for lack of an alternative? The answer is no: I could have been a lawyer or full-time university teacher, I had youthful dreams of the diplomatic corps, I had some mathematical ability... the only area where I would be useless would have been commerce.

Moshe Rabbenu, the first rabbi, said, "How can I bear unaided your trouble, your burden and your strife?" (Deut. 1:12). He carried a heavy load and got little rest, but the people irked him with their unbelief and disunity. Today the complaints are the same. Plus another: the other rabbis. On the Purim page of the *Jewish Chronicle*, Chaim Bermant defined a rabbi: "*Rav* = rabbi, from *riv*, to quarrel". Rabbis attacked me for mixing too much with Christian clergy, spending too much time at universities, not having a big enough beard. Some were aghast if they saw a picture of me with a reform rabbi. One rabbi was heard to say, "Rabbi Apple should be chucked out!"

Was I right to be a rabbi? A rabbi expects to be the communal sage-in-residence; the community expect him to be their surrogate saint. Nothing stops them from blaming the rabbi for everything and in some congregations the rabbi blames the congregation for everything. In the first year in some places, the rabbi is idolised, in the second he is terrorised and in the third marginalised. Some rabbis burn out, wear out and get out. This rabbi verged on burn-out, but he stayed the distance.

He enjoyed most of what he did. He accentuated the positive. He had an amazing array of opportunities to speak of and for Judaism. He valued being the Jewish presence in the public arena. He had many exhilarating moments. His heart and mind were constantly stretched. Would he choose this profession again? Some people fall into the rabbinate; I chose it. I recall my Masonic mentor Harry Kellerman, who wanted to be a teacher and worked hard to persuade his father to approve. The father said, "Allright, so be a teacher: but be the best possible kind of teacher that you can". I chose to be a rabbi, and tried to be the best possible kind of rabbi that I could.

GLOSSARY

Ahad HaAm – Asher Ginzberg, Zionist author
Aliyah (pl. **Aliyot**) – ascent to Torah reading or to live in Israel
Av Beth Din – head of rabbinical court
Avinu Shebashamayim – "Our Father in Heaven"
Avodah Zarah – idolatry
Avodat Yisra'el – a liturgical work
Ba'al Keri'ah – public Torah reader
Ba'al Shem Tov – founder of Hassidism
Ba'al Simhah – one celebrating a happy event
Ba'al Teki'ah – *shofar* blower
Barmitzvah/Batmitzvah – child at religious majority
Ben – son (of)
Bet Hillel, Bet Shammai – rival schools of sages
Bet(h) Din – rabbinical court
B'nei Akiva –youth group
B'rakhah – benediction
Chabad – Hassidic sect
Chaver (pl. **Chaverim**) – friend
Chavurata Kadishta – holy brotherhood
Cholent (pron. **Tcholent**) – stew cooked overnight
Day(y)an – rabbinical judge
D'var Torah - Torah exposition
Etrog – citron for Sukkot festival

Fleishig (Yiddish) – containing meat
Frum/froom (Yiddish) – pious, orthodox
Gabbai – synagogue warden
Ga'on – genius
Gedolei Ha-Dor – great scholars of the age
Gelilah – binding the Torah scroll
Gehinnom – hell
Haftarah – reading from Prophets
Hagbahah – raising the Torah scroll
Halakhah – Jewish law
HaRav – the rabbi
Haredi – highly orthodox
Hassid – pietist
Haz(z)an – cantor
Herem – ban, excommunication
Hesped – eulogy
JNF – Jewish National Fund
Kaddish – prayer usually said by mourners
Kaddish D'Rabbanan – prayer after studying rabbinic texts
Kashrut – dietary ("kosher") laws
Kiddushin – betrothal
Kippah – skull cap
Kohen (pl. **Kohanim**) – descendant of Biblical priests
Kohen Tzedek – righteous priest
Lamed-Vavnik – one of 36 saints of the age
Levi – descendant of Biblical Levites
Mah Nishtanah – Passover night questions
Mahzor – festival prayer book
Mezuzah – prayer roll on doorpost
Midrash – exposition, usually homiletical
Mishnah – law code
Mitzvah (pl. **Mitzvot**), commandment, good deed
Moshe Rabbenu – Moses our Teacher
Musaph – additional service on Sabbath and festivals
Ner Tamid – eternal lamp in synagogue
OH – *Orah Hayyim*, part of Jewish law code
Oisgehangene (Yiddish) – hanging down
Olam HaBa – afterlife

Olim – immigrants to Israel
Or Hadash – "new light"; a Sydney synagogue
Pareve – without meat or dairy content
Pesah – Passover
Pir'kei Avot – Ethics of the Fathers
Rambam – Moses Maimonides, medieval thinker
Rav – rabbi
Reshei Galuta – exilarchs; early medieval leaders
Rosh HaShanah – New Year
Sefer – book, scroll
Shabbat/Shabbos/Shobbos – Sabbath
Shammas(h) – beadle
Shavu'ot - Pentecost
Shehitah – slaughter of animals (by *shohet*) for food
Shema – declaration of faith
Shtender (Yiddish) – prayer or study lectern
Shtiebel (Yiddish) – prayer room
Shir HaShirim – Song of Songs
Shirat HaYam – Song of the Sea (Ex. 15)
Shi'ur (pl. **Shi'urim**) – study session
Shivah – week of mourning
Shofar – ram's horn trumpet on New Year
Shule (Yiddish) – synagogue
Siddur – prayer book
Simhah – celebration
Simhat Torah – Torah festival
Sukkah – harvest booth on festival of Sukkot
Tallit – prayer shawl
Talmid Hakham – rabbinic scholar
Talmud – corpus of rabbinic learning
Tanakh – Hebrew Bible
Tanhuma – a midrashic work
Tef(ph)illin – prayer boxes worn by males at morning worship
Tehillim – Psalms
Tikkun Leil Shavu'ot – all-night study on Shavu'ot
Tisha B'Av – fast commemorating the Temple
Torah – 5 Books of Moses; Jewish knowledge
Tzaddik (pl. **Tzaddikim**) – righteous person

Tzitzit – fringes
Yahrzeit (Yiddish) – anniversary of death
Yeshivah – Talmudic college
Yimma<u>h</u> shemam – "May their names be erased"
Yizkor – memorial prayer on festivals
Yomtov (colloquially **Yuntif**) – festival
Zoll zein (Yiddish) – "let there be"
Zohar – medieval mystical commentary

PRONUNCIATION: ch/<u>h</u>/kh = "ch" in Scottish "loch"

THE AUTHOR

For many years the author of this book, Rabbi Raymond Apple, was the leading Australian rabbi and an Australian national figure.

Born and educated in Melbourne, he went to Britain as a student and gained a minister's diploma, teacher's diploma and rabbinic ordination at Jews' College (the London School of Jewish Studies). He also has qualifications in arts, law, history, religion and education, and holds honorary doctorates from two Australian universities and awards from two others. After serving as religious director of the Association of Jewish Youth in Britain, he ministered to London synagogues at Bayswater and Hampstead, and was also chairman of the Jewish Marriage Council, president of the Union of Anglo-Jewish Preachers, and a member of the Chief Rabbi's Cabinet.

From 1972 to 2005 he was senior rabbi of the Great Synagogue, Sydney. He was also senior rabbi to the Australian Defence Force, a member of the Sydney rabbinical court, a university teacher, Master of Mandelbaum House at Sydney University, mentor of many synagogues and organisations, and active in inter-community work.

He is patron and past chairman of the Australian Council of Christians and Jews, and Past Deputy Grand Master of the United Grand Lodge of New South Wales and the Australian Capital Territory. He is patron and past president of the Australian Jewish Historical Society, and life rabbinic governor and past president of the Australian and New Zealand orthodox rabbinate. He is an Officer of the Order of Australia and holds other awards including the Gold Medal of the International Council of Christians and Jews.

His weekly *OzTorah* has a world-wide email circulation; his books include *OzTorah* selections and memoirs entitled "To Be Continued". His papers on history and the Bible are regularly published in academic journals. He has written two books of Masonic scholarship.

He now lives in Israel and is engaged in research, writing and teaching. He and his wife Marian have four children as well as a number of grandchildren and great-grandchildren.

Lightning Source UK Ltd.
Milton Keynes UK
UKOW03f0708211014

240409UK00003B/207/P

9 781496 992239